IRISH BALLADS

piano
vocal
guitar

T0084124

ISBN-13: 978-1-4234-1137-6

HAL•LEONARD®
CORPORATION
7777 W. BLUEMOUND RD. P.O. BOX 13819 MILWAUKEE, WI 53213

In Australia Contact:
Hal Leonard Australia Pty. Ltd.
4 Lentara Court
Cheltenham East, 3192 Victoria, Australia
Email: ausadmin@halleonard.com

Visit Hal Leonard Online at
www.halleonard.com

CONTENTS

5	Arthur McBride
8	The Bard of Armagh
10	Believe Me, If All Those Endearing Young Charms
12	Black Velvet Band
20	Boston Burglar
17	Botany Bay
22	Boulavogue
28	Brennan on the Moor
30	Butcher Boy
25	Carrickfergus
32	Cliffs of Doneen
38	The Croppy Boy
40	Danny Boy
42	Down by the Salley Gardens
35	Easy and Slow
44	Finnegan's Wake
48	The Foggy Dew
50	Green Grow the Rashes, O
52	Henry My Son
54	I Know My Love
47	I Know Where I'm Goin'
56	I Never Will Marry
58	I'll Tell Me Ma
60	I'm a Rover and Seldom Sober
62	Johnny I Hardly Knew Ye
64	Jug of Punch
66	Lark in the Morning
70	Leaving of Liverpool
72	The Meeting of the Waters
74	The Mermaid
78	Minstrel Boy
80	Molly Malone (Cockles & Mussels)
82	The Mountains of Mourne
85	My Singing Bird
88	A Nation Once Again
94	O'Donnell Aboo
91	The Patriot Game
96	The Raggle-Taggle Gypsy
98	Red Is the Rose
103	The Rocks of Bawn
106	The Rocky Road to Dublin
110	Roddy McCorley
112	The Rose of Tralee
118	Rosin the Bow
122	Sam Hall
124	Skibbereen
126	The Snowy-Breasted Pearl
128	The Spanish Lady
130	Star of County Down
132	Sweet Carnlough Bay
68	Tis the Last Rose of Summer
134	The Wearing of the Green
115	Whiskey in the Jar
136	The Wild Colonial Boy
139	Wild Rover

ARTHUR McBRIDE

Traditional Irish Folk Song

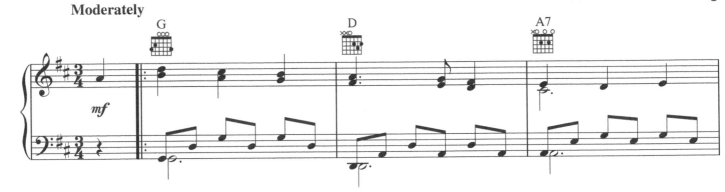

I had a first cous - in called
He says, "My young fel - lows, if

Ar - thur Mc - Bride. He and I took a
you will en - list, a guin - ea you

stroll down ____ by the sea - side, a -
quick - ly shall have in your ___ fist. Be -

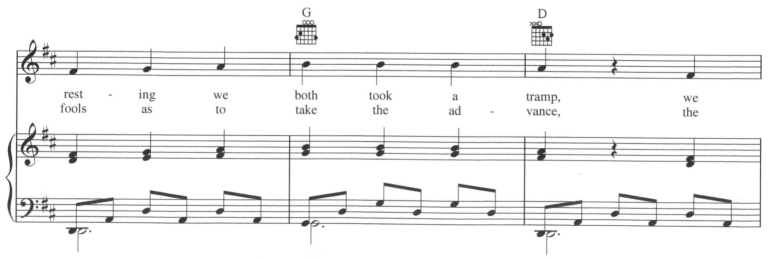

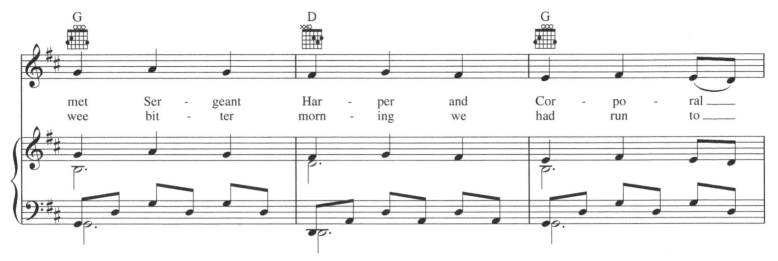

met Ser - geant Har - per and Cor - po - ral _____
wee bit - ter morn - ing and we had run to _____

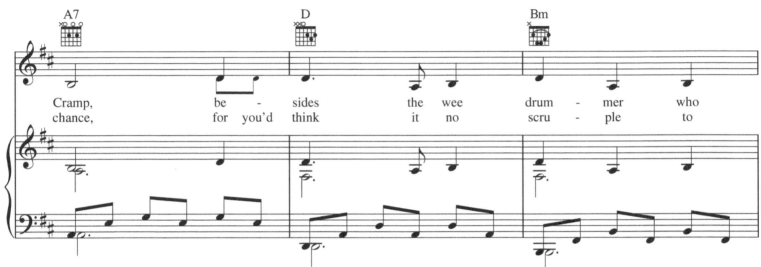

Cramp, be - sides the wee drum - mer who
chance, for you'd think it no scru - ple to

beat up for camp, with his row - dy - dow -
send us to France, where __ we would be

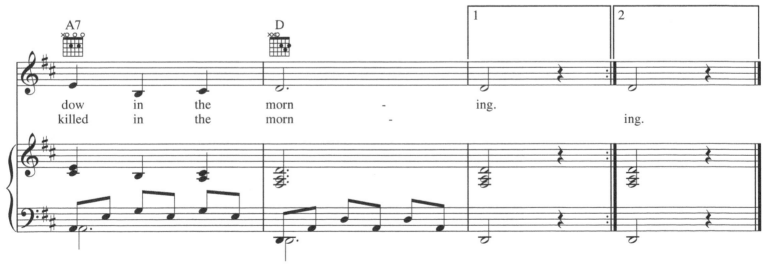

dow in the morn - ing.
killed in the morn - ing.

THE BARD OF ARMAGH

Traditional Irish Folk Song

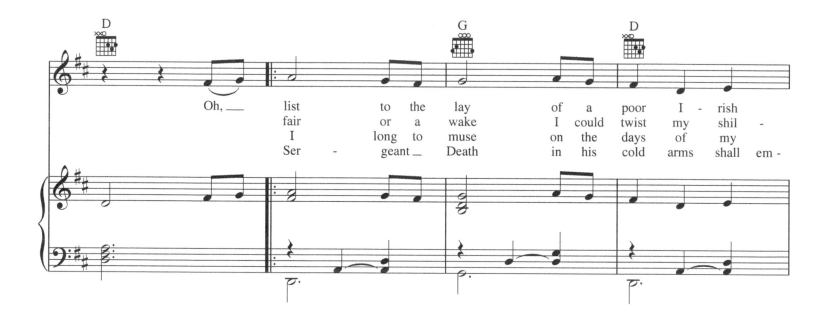

Oh, ___ list to the lay of a poor I - rish
fair or a wake I could twist my shil -
I long to muse on the days of my
Ser - geant ___ Death in his cold arms shall em -

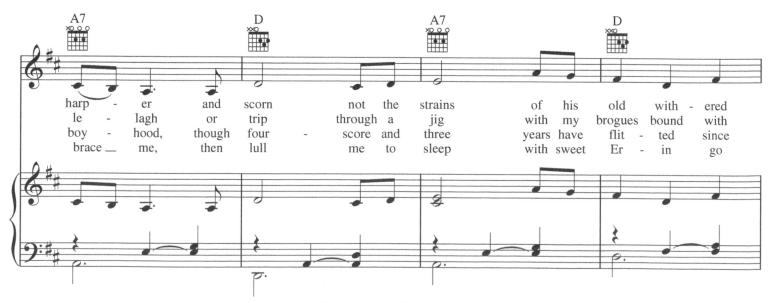

harp - er and scorn not the strains of his old with - ered
le - lagh or trip through a jig with my brogues bound with
boy - hood, though four - score and three years have flit - ted since
brace ___ me, then lull me to sleep with sweet Er - in go

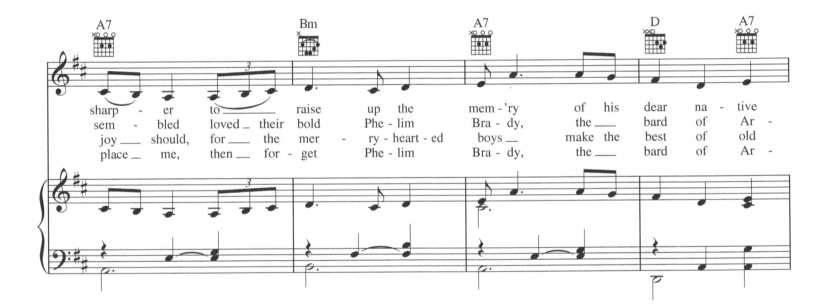

BELIEVE ME, IF ALL THOSE ENDEARING YOUNG CHARMS

Words and Music by
THOMAS MOORE

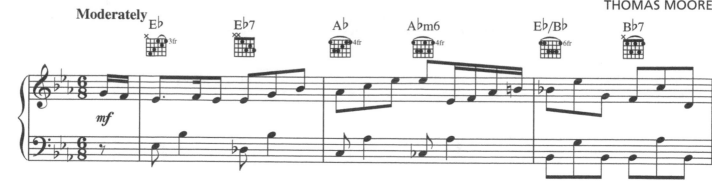

BLACK VELVET BAND

Traditional Irish Folk Song

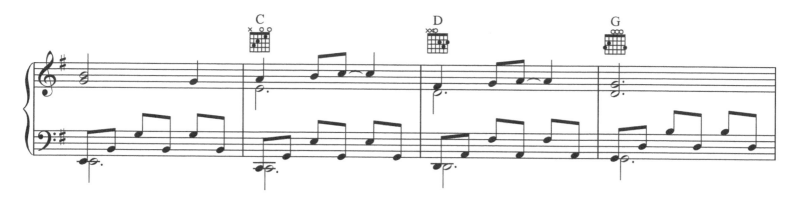

Her eyes they shun like _____ dia - monds; _____ you'd think she was queen of the land. _____

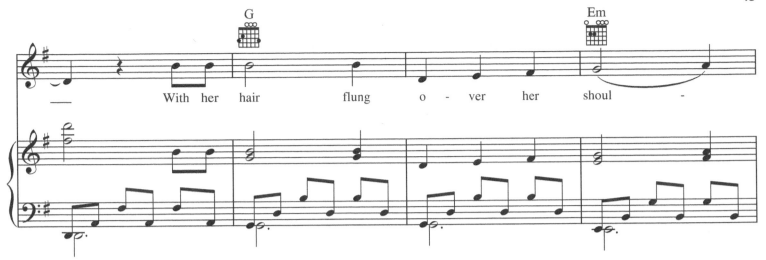

With her hair flung o - ver her shoul -

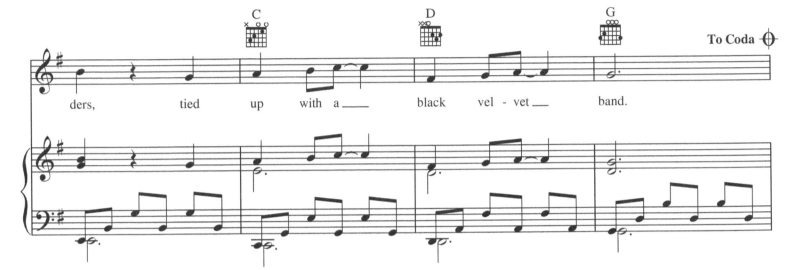

To Coda ⊕

ders, tied up with a black vel - vet band.

As I went walk - ing down Broad - way,
'Fore judge and ju - ry next morn - ing

not in - tend - ing to stay ver - y long,
both of us did ap - pear.

I met with this __ frol - ick - some dam -
A gen - tle - man __ claimed his _____ jew - el -

sel __ as she _____ came trip - ping a - long. _____
ry and the case a - gainst us was clear. _____

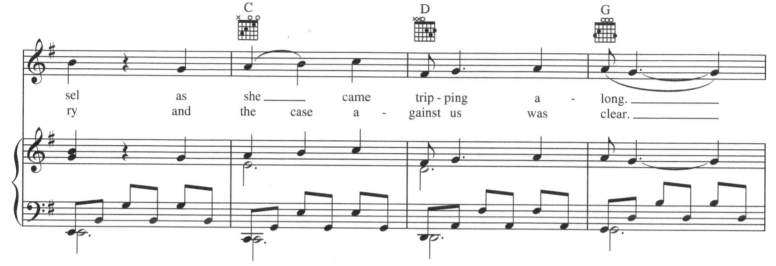

A watch she pulled out __ of her __ pock - et _____
Sev - en long years __ trans - por - ta - tion _____

and slipped it right __ in - to me __ hand. _____
right on down to __ Van Die - men's _ Land; _____

On the ver-y first day that I ____ met _____
far a-way from my friends and com - pan -

her, bad luck to her ____ black vel - vet ____
ions to fol - low the ___ black vel - vet ____

D.S. al Coda

1.
G
band. Her

2.
G
band. Her

CODA

Her eyes they shun like _____

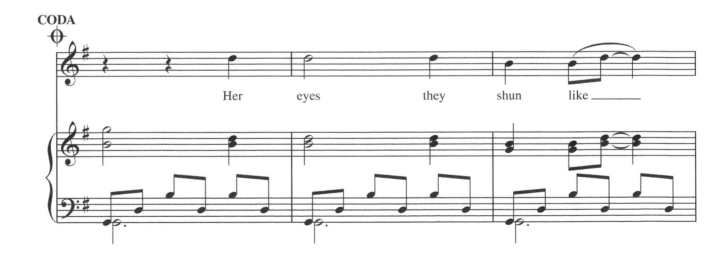

16

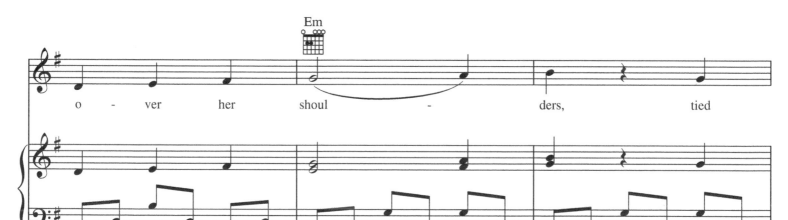

BOTANY BAY

Australian Folk Song

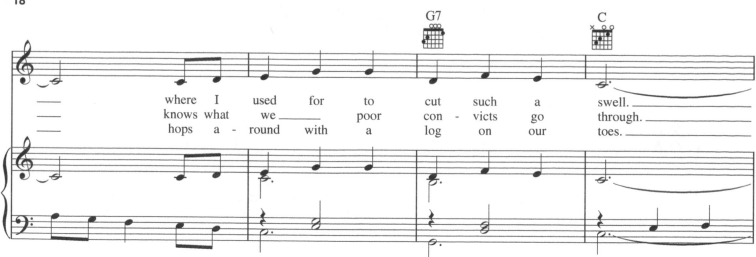

where I used for to cut such a swell.
knows what we ___ to poor con- victs go through.
hops a- round with a log on our toes.

Refrain

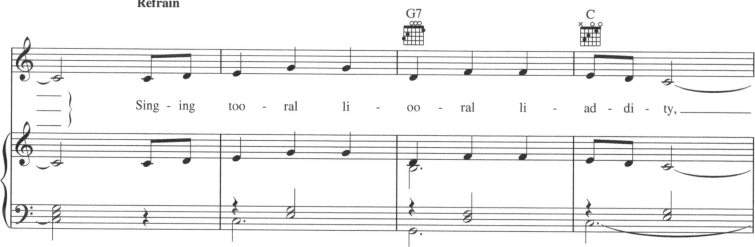

Sing- ing too- ral li- oo- ral li- ad- di- ty, ___

sing- ing too- ral li- oo- ral li- ay. ___

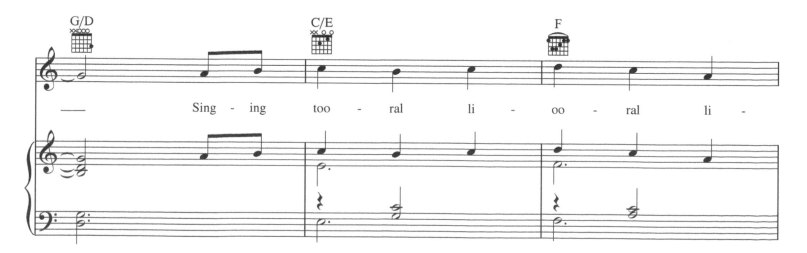

Sing- ing too- ral li- oo- ral li-

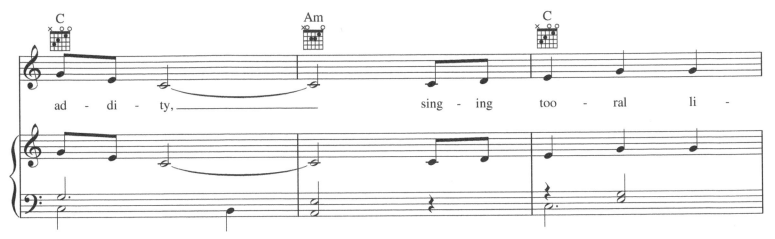

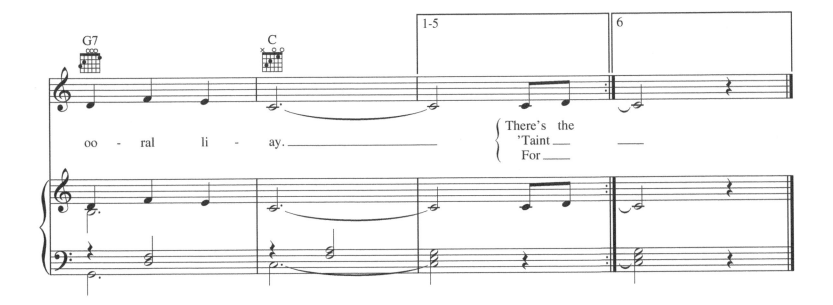

Additional Lyrics

4. For seven long years I'll be staying here,
   For seven long years and a day.
   For meeting a cove in an area
   And taking his ticker away.
   Refrain

5. Oh, had I the wings of a turtle dove!
   I'd soar on my pinions so high.
   Slap bang to the arms of my Polly love,
   And in her sweet presence I'd die.
   Refrain

6. Now, all my young Dookies and Duchesses,
   Take warning from what I've to say.
   Mind all is your own as you touchesses.
   Or you'll find us in Botany Bay.
   Refrain

BOSTON BURGLAR

Traditional Irish Folk Song

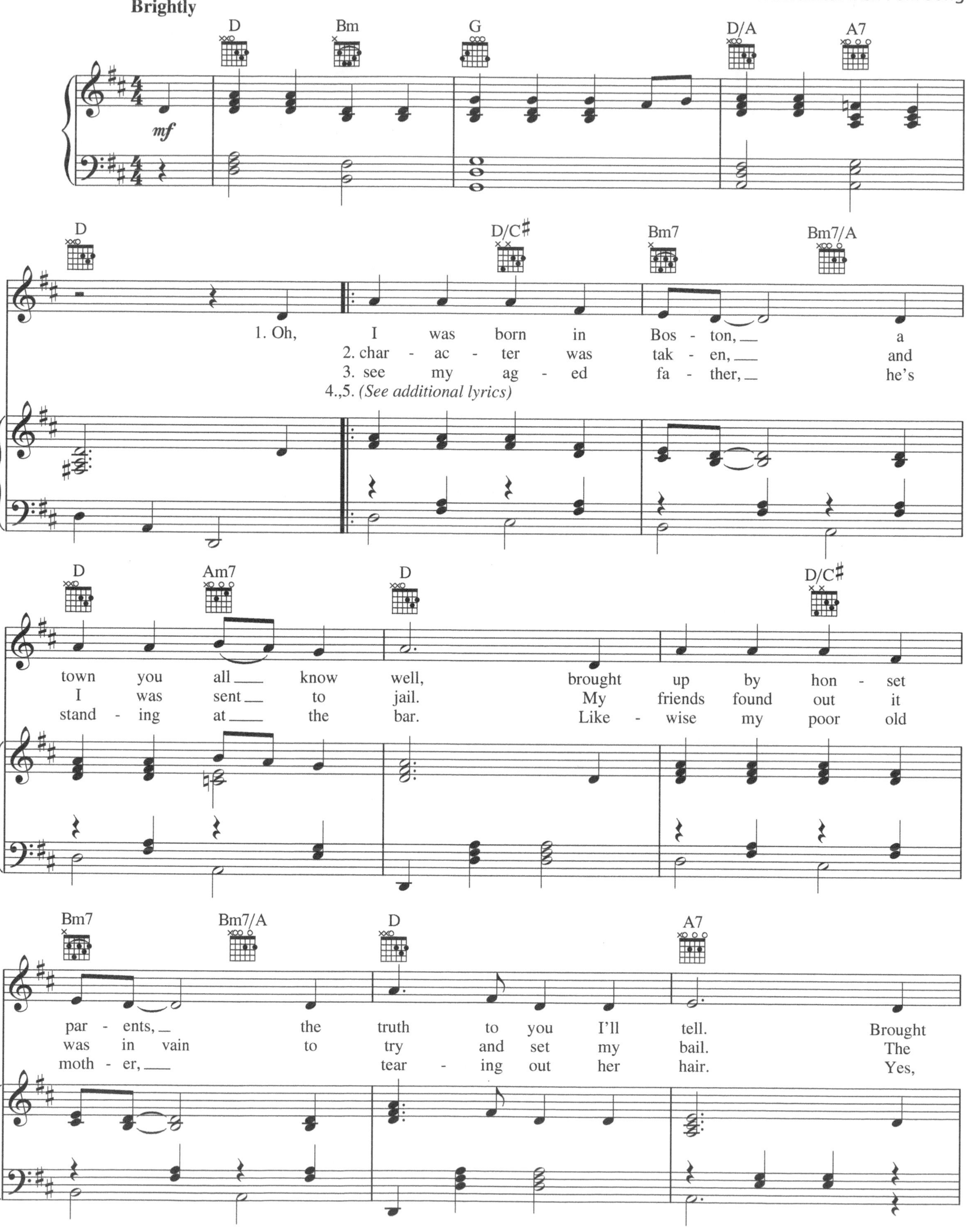

Brightly
D Bm G D/A A7
mf
D D/C# Bm7 Bm7/A
1. Oh, I was born in Bos - ton, a
2. char - ac - ter was tak - en, and
3. see my ag - ed fa - ther, he's
4.,5. (See additional lyrics)
D Am7 D D/C#
town you all know well, brought up by hon - set
I was sent to jail. My friends found out it
stand - ing at the bar. Like - wise my poor old
Bm7 Bm7/A D A7
par - ents, the truth to you I'll tell. Brought
was in vain to try and set my bail. The
moth - er, tear - ing out her hair. Yes,

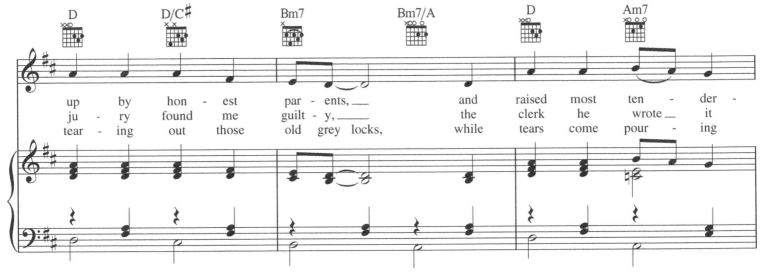

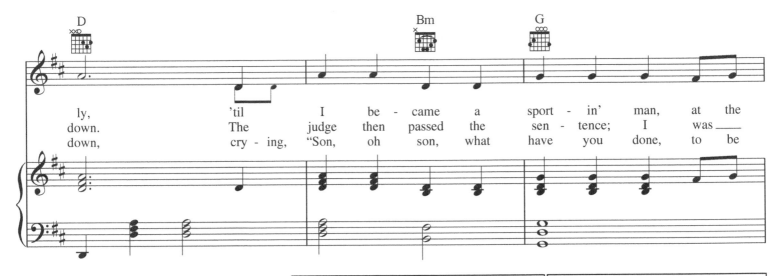

Additional Lyrics

4. I was put on board an eastern train, one cold December day.
   And ev'ry station that we passed I'd hear the people say,
   "There goes the Boston burglar. In strong chains he is bound.
   For some crime or another, he is going to Charlestown."

5. Now there's a girl in Boston, a girl that I love well.
   And when I gain my freedom, along with her I'll dwell.
   Yes, when I gain my freedom, bad company I'll shun.
   Likewise night walking, rambling, and also drinking rum.

BOULAVOGUE

Irish Folk Song
Words and Music by P.J. McCALL

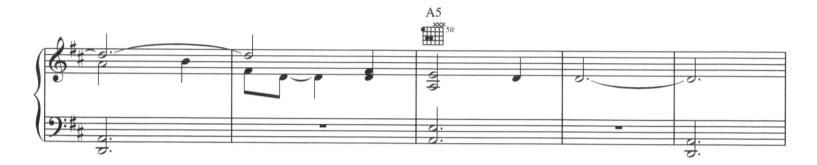

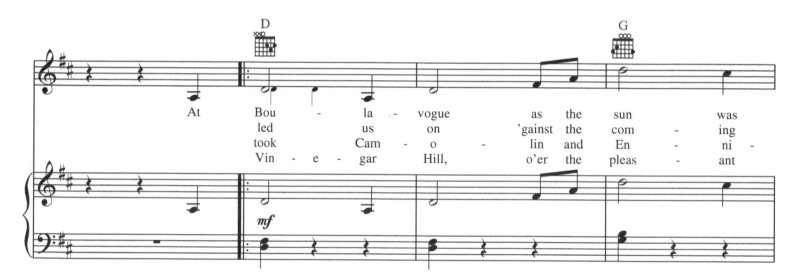

At Bou - la - vogue as the sun was
led us on 'gainst the com - ing
took Cam - o - lin and En - ni -
Vin - e - gar Hill, o'er the pleas - ant

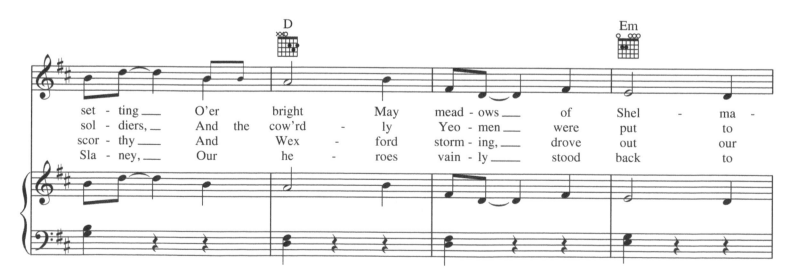

set - ting ___ O'er bright May mead - ows ___ of Shel - ma -
sol - diers, ___ And the cow'rd - ly Yeo - men ___ were put to
scor - thy ___ And Wex - ford storm - ing, ___ drove out our
Sla - ney, ___ Our he - roes vain - ly ___ stood back to

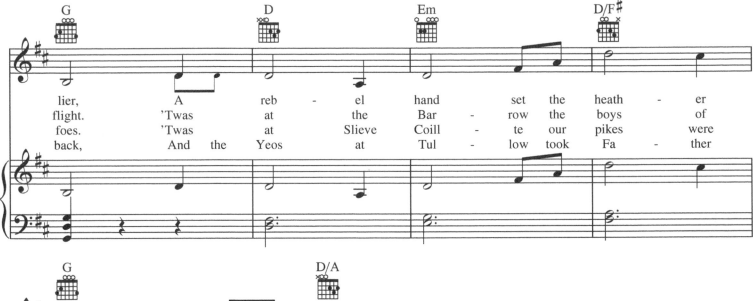

lier, A reb - el hand set the heath - er
flight. 'Twas at the Bar - row the boys of
foes. 'Twas at Slieve Coill - te our pikes were
back, And the Yeos at Tul - low took Fa - ther

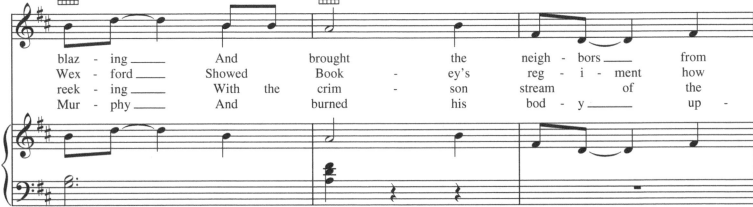

blaz - ing ____ And brought the neigh - bors ____ from
Wex - ford ____ Showed Book - ey's reg - i - ment how
reek - ing ____ With the crim - son stream of the
Mur - phy ____ And burned his bod - y ____ up -

far and near. ____ Then Fa - ther
men could fight. ____ Look out for
beat - en Yeos. ____ At Tub - ber -
on the rack. ____ God grant you

Mur - phy ____ from old Kil - cor - mack ____ Spurred up the
hire - lings, ____ King George of Eng - land, ____ Search ev - 'ry
neer - ing ____ and Bal - ly - el - lis ____ Full man - y a
glo - ry, ____ brave Fa - ther Mur - phy, ____ And o - pen

CARRICKFERGUS

Traditional Irish Folk Song

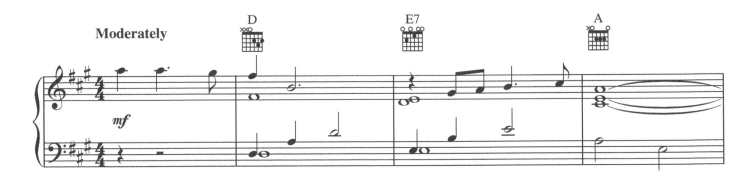

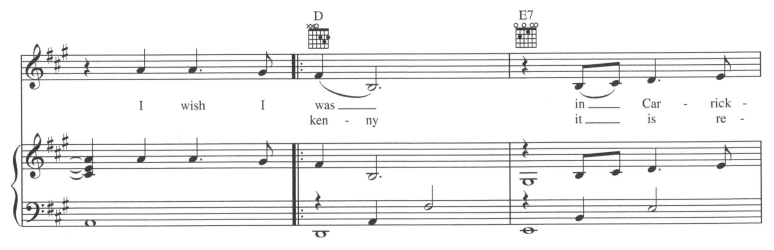

I wish I was
ken - ny   in ___ Car - rick - re -

fer - gus, ___   on - ly for   nights ___
port - ed, ___   they've mar - ble   stones ___

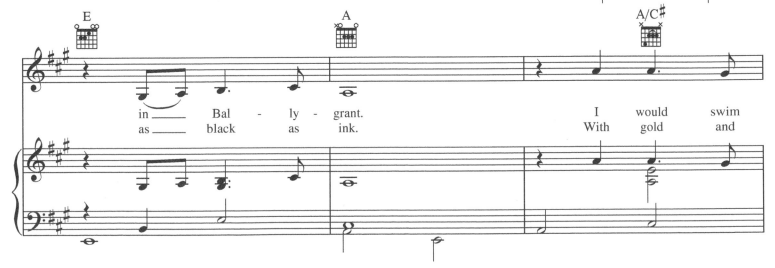

in ___ Bal - ly - grant.   I would swim and
as ___ black as   ink.   With gold and

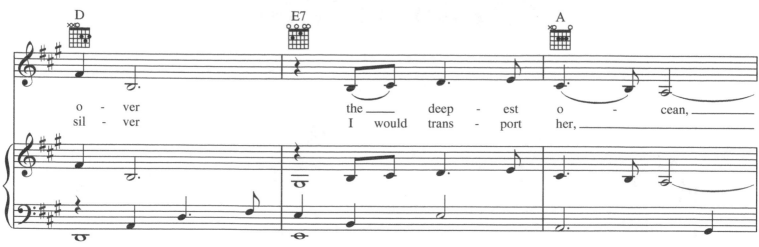

o - ver   the ___ deep - est o - cean, ___
sil - ver   I would trans - port her, _____

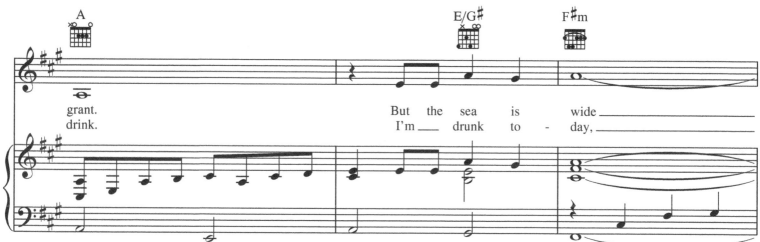

___ on - ly for nights ___ in ___ Bal - ly -
but I'll sing no more now 'til I get a

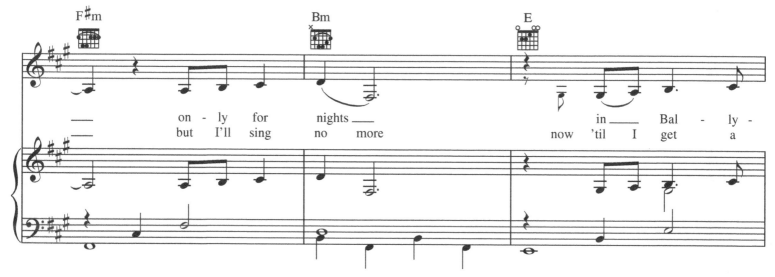

grant. But the sea is wide _____
drink. I'm ___ drunk to - day, _____

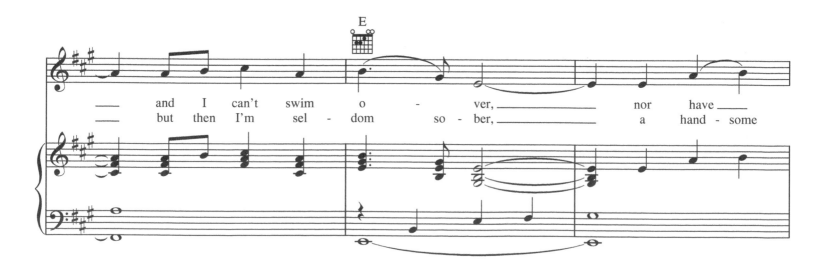

___ and I can't swim o - ver, _____ nor have ___
but then I'm sel - dom so - ber, _____ a hand - some

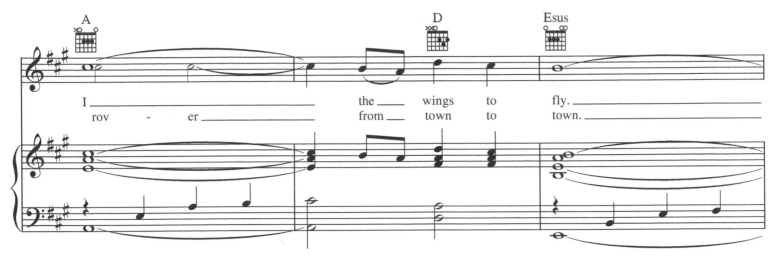

I _____ the ___ wings to fly. _____
rov - er _____ from ___ town to town. _____

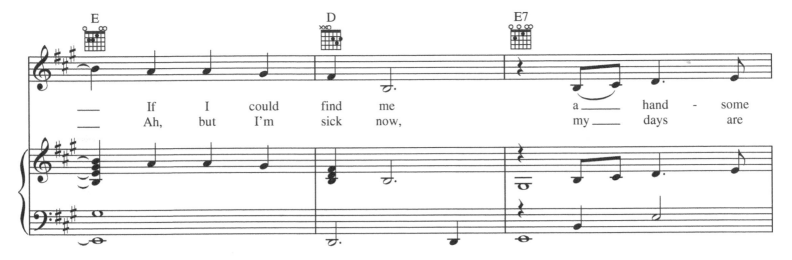

___ If I could find me a _____ hand - some
___ Ah, but I'm sick me now, my ___ days are

boats - man _____ to fer - ry me o - ver to my love and
o - ver. _____ Come all ye young lads, ___ and ___ lay me

die. Now in Kil - down.

BRENNAN ON THE MOOR

Traditional Irish Folk Song

Moderately

1. It's a-bout a fierce high-way-man my sto-ry I will tell.
2. up-on the King's high-way Old Bren-nan he sat down.
3. Bren-nan's wife had gone to town pro-vi-sions for to buy,

4.-6. *(See additional lyrics)*

His name was Wil-ly Bren-nan and in Ire-land he did dwell.
He met the may-or of Moor-land five miles out-side of town.
and when she saw her Wil-ly tak-en she be-gan to cry.

'Twas up-on the King's own moun-tain he be-gan his wild ca-reer, and
Now the may-or, he had heard of Bren-nan and, "I think," says he, "Your
Says he, "Hand me that ten-pen-ny," and as soon as Wil-ly spoke, she

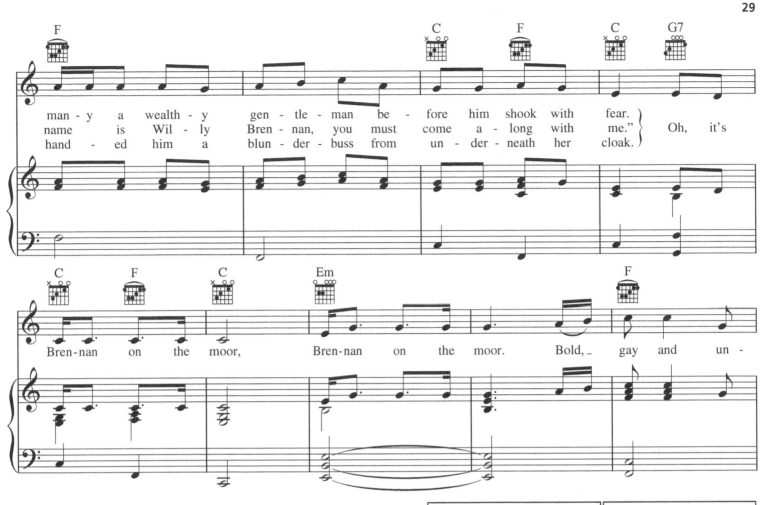

man - y a wealth - y gen - tle - man be - fore him shook with fear.
name is Wil - ly Bren - nan, you must come a - long with me." Oh, it's
hand - ed him a blun - der - buss from un - der - neath her cloak.

Bren - nan on the moor, Bren - nan on the moor. Bold, _ gay and un -

daunt - ed stood young Bren - nan on the moor. It was moor.
Now __
Now __

Additional Lyrics

4. Now Brennan got his blunderbuss, my story I'll unfold.
He caused the mayor to tremble and deliver up his gold.
Five thousand pounds were offered for his apprehension there,
But Brennan and the peddler to the mountain did repair.
Oh, it's Brennan on the moor, Brennan on the moor.
Bold, gay and undaunted stood young Brennan on the moor.

5. Now Brennan is an outlaw all on some mountain high.
With infantry and cavalry to take him they did try.
But he laughed at them and he scorned at them until, it was said,
By a false-hearted woman he was cruelly betrayed.
Oh, it's Brennan on the moor, Brennan on the moor.
Bold, gay and undaunted stood young Brennan on the moor.

6. They hung him at the crossroads; in chains he swung and died.
But still they say that in the night some do see him ride.
They see him with his blunderbuss in the midnight chill;
Along, along the king's highway rides Willy Brennan still.
Oh, it's Brennan on the moor, Brennan on the moor.
Bold, gay and undaunted stood young Brennan on the moor.

BUTCHER BOY

Traditional Irish Folk Song

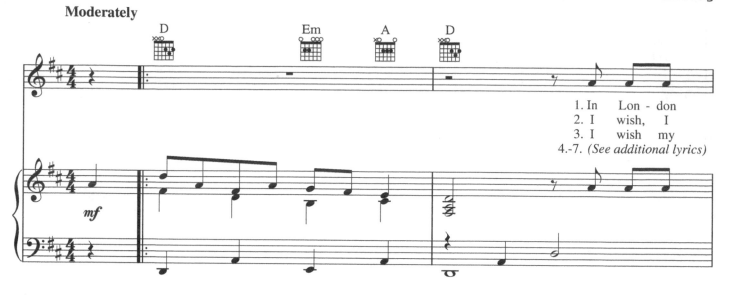

Moderately

1. In Lon - don
2. I wish, I
3. I wish my
4.-7. *(See additional lyrics)*

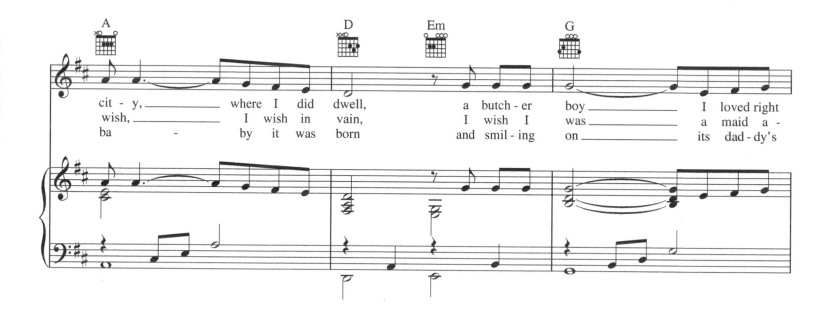

cit - y, _____ where I did dwell, a butch - er boy _____ I loved right
wish, _____ I wish in vain, I wish I was _____ a maid a -
ba - by it was born and smil - ing on _____ its dad - dy's

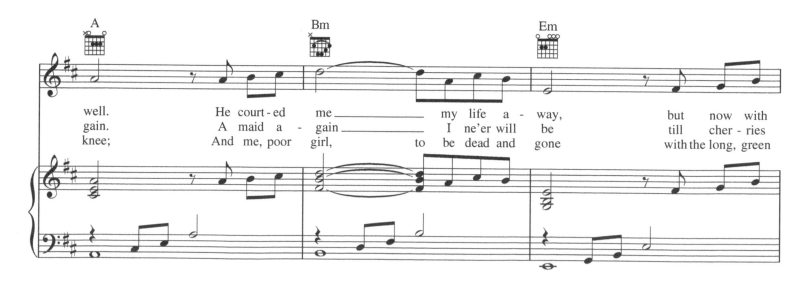

well. He court - ed me _____ my life a - way, but now with
gain. A maid a - gain _____ I ne'er will be till cher - ries
knee; And me, poor girl, to be dead and gone with the long, green

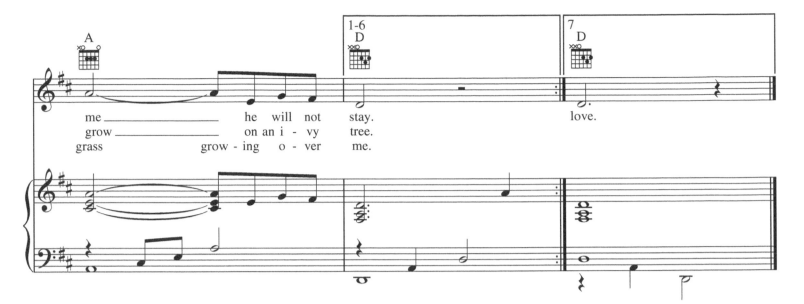

me _____ he will not stay.
grow _____ on an i - vy tree.
grass grow - ing o - ver me.

love.

Additional Lyrics

4. She went upstairs to go to bed,
   And calling to her mother said,
   "Give me a chair till I sit down
   And a pen and ink till I write down."

5. At ev'ry word she dropped a tear,
   At ev'ry line cried, "Willie, dear,
   Oh, what a foolish girl was I
   To be led astray by a butcher boy."

6. He went upstairs and the door he broke;
   He found her hanging from a rope.
   He took his knife and he cut her down,
   And in her pocket these words he found:

7. "Oh, make my grave large, wide and deep;
   Put a marble stone at my head and feet.
   And in the middle a turtledove,
   That the world may know that I died for love."

CLIFFS OF DONEEN

Traditional Irish Folk Song

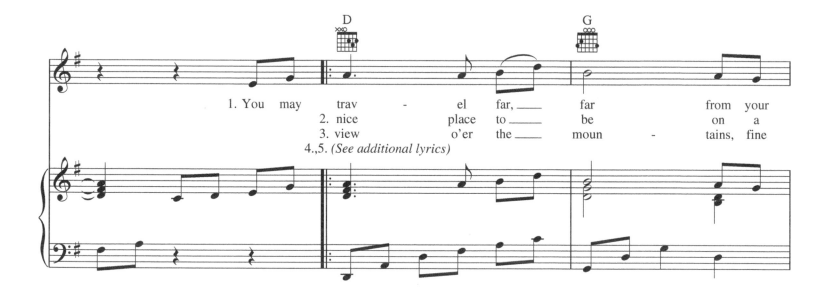

1. You may trav - el far, _____ far   from your
2. nice   place to _____ be   on a
3. view   o'er the _____ moun - tains, fine
4.,5. *(See additional lyrics)*

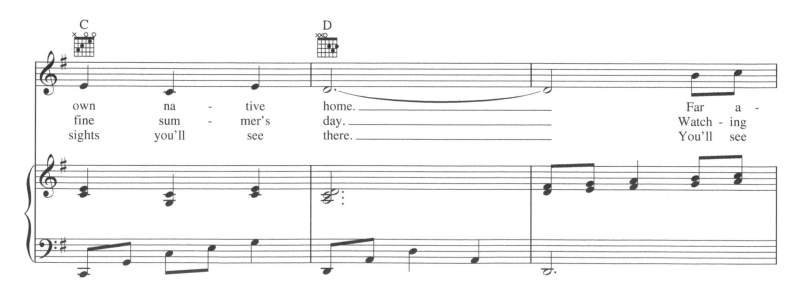

own   na - tive   home. _____   Far a -
fine sum - mer's   day. _____   Watch - ing
sights you'll   see   there. _____   You'll see

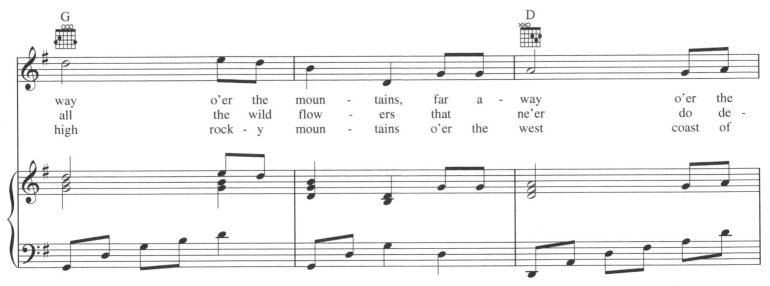

way o'er the moun - tains, far a - way o'er the
all the wild flow - ers that ne'er do de -
high rock - y moun - tains o'er the west coast of

foam. _____
cay. _____
Clare. _____

But of all the fine
Oh, the hares and the
Oh, the towns of Kil -

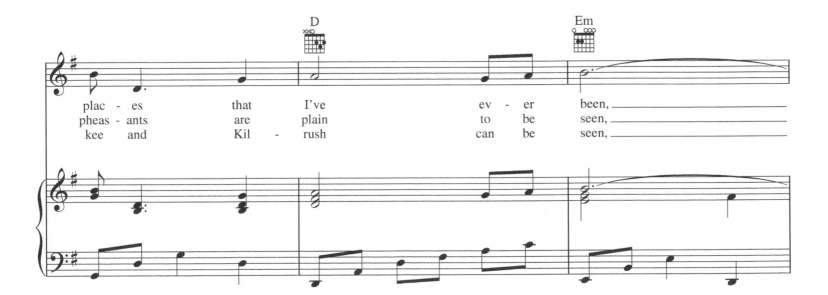

plac - es that I've ev - er been, _____
pheas - ants are plain to be seen, _____
kee and Kil - rush can be seen, _____

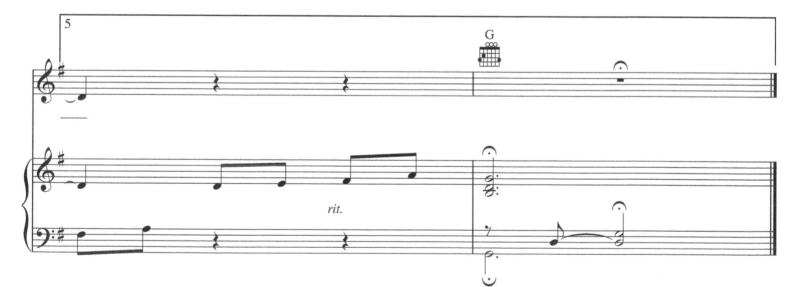

Additional Lyrics

4. Fare thee well to Doneen, fare thee well for a while
And to all the kind people I'm leaving behind.
To the streams and the meadows where late I have been,
And the high rocky slopes 'round the cliffs of Doneen.

5. Fare thee well to Doneen, fare thee well for a while.
And although we are parted by the raging sea wild,
Once again I will walk with my Irish colleen
'Round the high rocky slopes of the cliffs of Doneen.

EASY AND SLOW

Traditional Irish Folk Song

wheth - er or no. Wheth - er I'm eas - y or

wheth - er I'm true. _____ As she lift - ed her

pet - ti - coat eas - y and slow, And I rolled up my

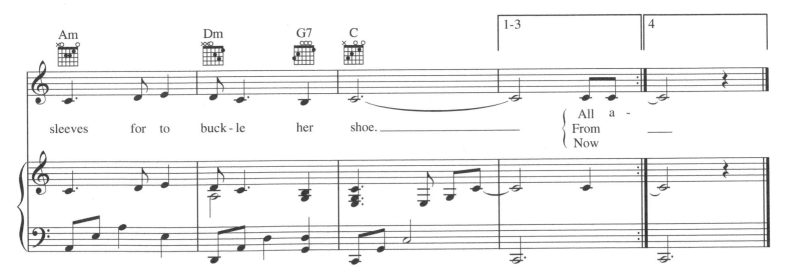

sleeves for to buck - le her shoe. _____

1-3   4

All a -
From
Now

THE CROPPY BOY

18th Century Irish Folk Song

Moderately

1. 'Twas ear - ly, ear - ly
2. ear - ly, ear - ly
3. in the guard - house where
4.-7. *(See additional lyrics)*

in in the spring, the birds did whis - tle and
in in the night, the yeo - man cav - al - ry
I was laid, and in the par - lor where

sweet - ly sing, _____ chang - ing their notes from
gave me a fright. The yeo - man cav - al - ry
I was tried. _____ My sen - tence passed and my

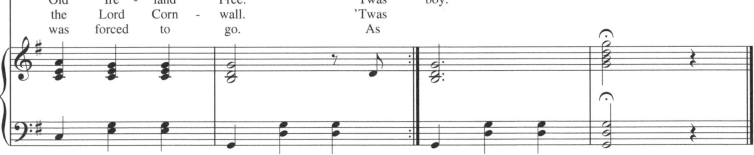

Additional Lyrics

4. As I was passing my father's door, my brother William stood at the door.
   My aged father stood there also, my tender mother her hair she tore.

5. As I was going up Wexford Hill, who could blame me to cry my fill?
   I looked behind and I looked before, my aged mother I shall see no more.

6. As I was mounted on the scaffold high, my aged father was standing by.
   My aged father did me deny, and the name he gave me was the croppy boy.

7. 'Twas in the Dungannon this young man died, and in Dungannon his body lies.
   And you good people that do pass by, oh, shed a tear for the croppy boy.

DANNY BOY
(Londonderry Air)

Words by FREDERICK EDWARD WEATHERLY
Traditional Irish Folk Melody

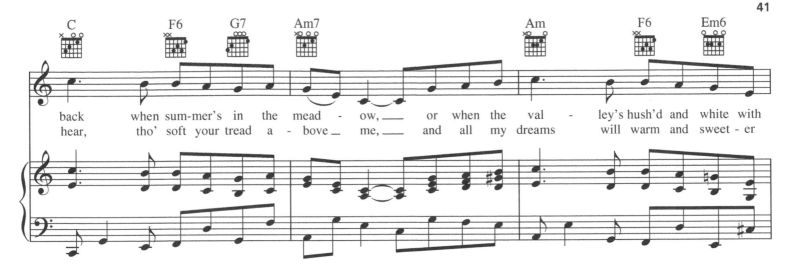

back, when sum-mer's in the mead - ow, ___ or when the val - ley's hush'd and white with
hear, tho' soft your tread a - bove ___ me, ___ and all my dreams will warm and sweet - er

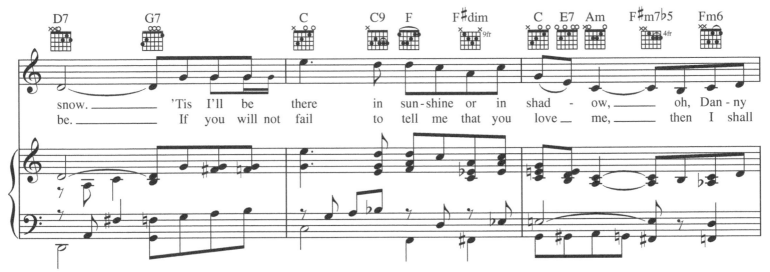

snow. _____ 'Tis I'll be there in sun-shine or in shad - ow, ___ oh, Dan - ny
be. _____ If you will not fail to tell me that you love ___ me, ___ then I shall

Boy, oh Dan - ny Boy, I love you so! ___
sleep in peace un - til you come to me!

But if ye

DOWN BY THE SALLEY GARDENS

Traditional Irish Folk Song

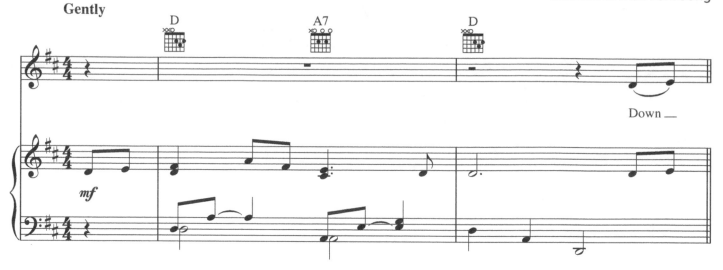

Down —

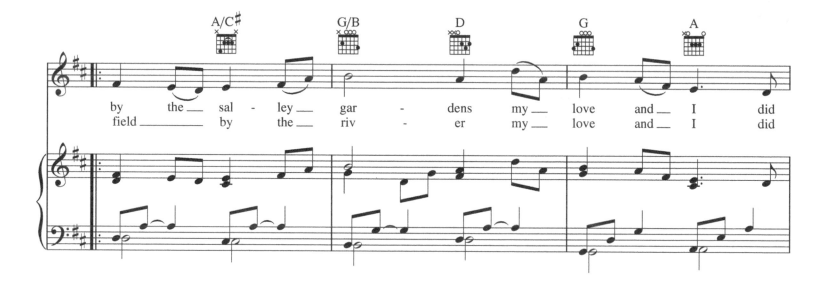

by the — sal — ley — gar - dens my — love and — I did
field — by the — riv - er my — love and — I did

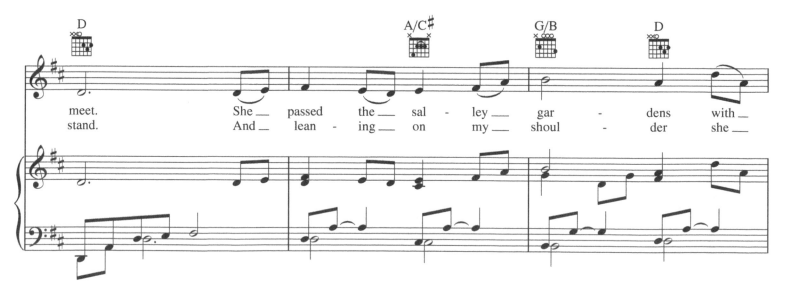

meet. She passed the — sal - ley — gar - dens with —
stand. And lean - ing — on my — shoul - der she —

lit - tle ___ snow - white feet.   She bid me ___ take love
laid her ___ snow - white hand.   She bid me ___ take life

eas - y,   as the leaves grow ___ on ___ the ___ tree.   But ___
eas - y,   as the grass grows ___ on ___ the ___ weirs.   But ___

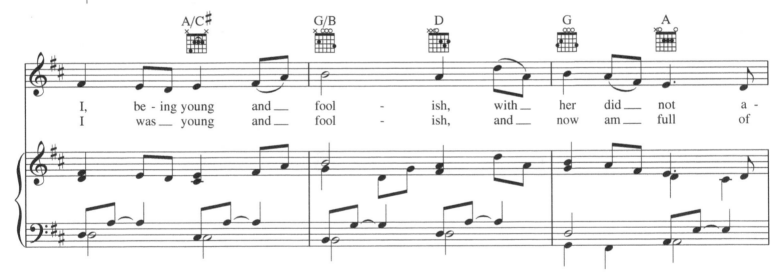

I,   be - ing young and ___ fool - ish,   with ___ her did ___ not a -
I was ___ young and ___ fool - ish,   and ___ now am ___ full of

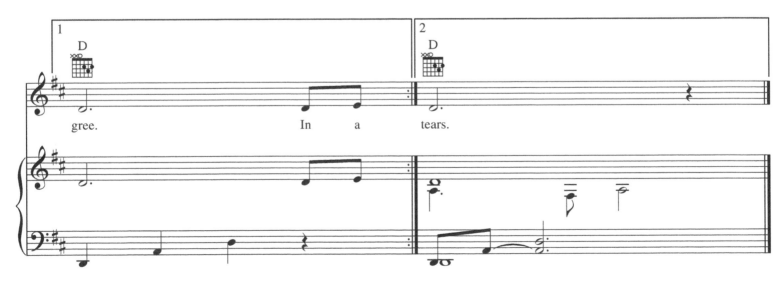

gree.   In a   tears.

FINNEGAN'S WAKE

Traditional Irish Folk Song

Moderately

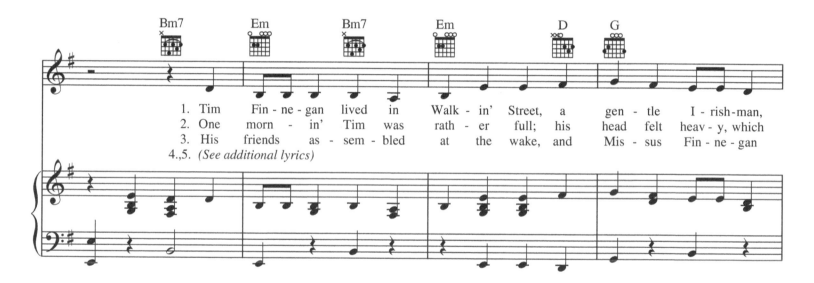

1. Tim Fin - ne - gan lived in Walk - in' Street, a gen - tle I - rish-man,
2. One morn - in' Tim was rath - er full; his head felt heav - y, which
3. His friends as - sem - bled at the wake, and Mis - sus Fin - ne - gan
4.,5. *(See additional lyrics)*

might - y odd. He had a brogue both rich and sweet, and to
made him shake. He fell from a lad - der and he broke his skull, and they
called for lunch. ___ First they brought in tay and cake, then ___

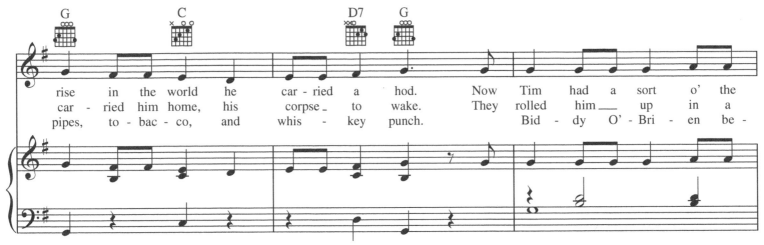

rise in the world he car - ried a hod. Now Tim had a sort o' the
car - ried him home, his corpse to wake. They rolled him up in a
pipes, to - bac - co, and whis - key punch. Bid - dy O' - Bri - en be -

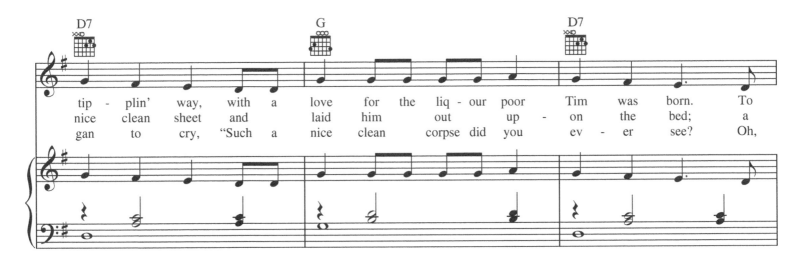

tip - plin' way, with a love for the liq - our poor Tim was born. To
nice clean sheet and laid him out up - on the bed; a
gan to cry, "Such a nice clean corpse did you ev - er see? Oh,

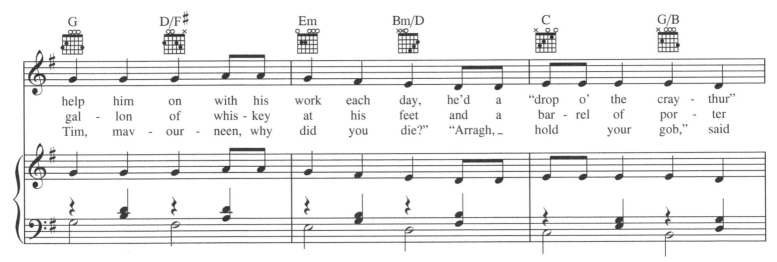

help him on with his work each day, he'd a "drop o' the cray - thur"
gal - lon of whis - key at his feet and a bar - rel of por - ter
Tim, mav - our - neen, why did you die?" "Arragh, hold your gob," said

Chorus

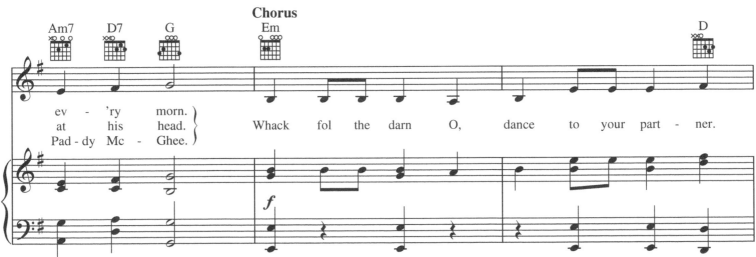

ev - 'ry morn.
at his head.
Pad - dy Mc - Ghee.

Whack fol the darn O, dance to your part - ner.

Additional Lyrics

4. Then Maggie O'Connor took up the job,
   "Oh Biddy," says she, "you're wrong, I'm sure."
   Biddy, she gave her a belt in the gob
   And left her sprawlin' on the floor.
   And then the war did soon engage,
   'Twas woman to woman and man to man.
   Shillelaigh law was all the rage,
   And a row and ruction soon began.
   Chorus

5. Then Mickey Maloney ducked his head
   When a noggin of whiskey flew at him.
   It missed, and falling on the bed,
   The liquor scattered over Tim!
   The corpse revives; see how he rises!
   Timothy, rising from the bed,
   Said, "Whirl your whiskey around like blazes,
   Thanum an Dhul! Do you think I'm dead?"
   Chorus

I KNOW WHERE I'M GOIN'

English Folk Song

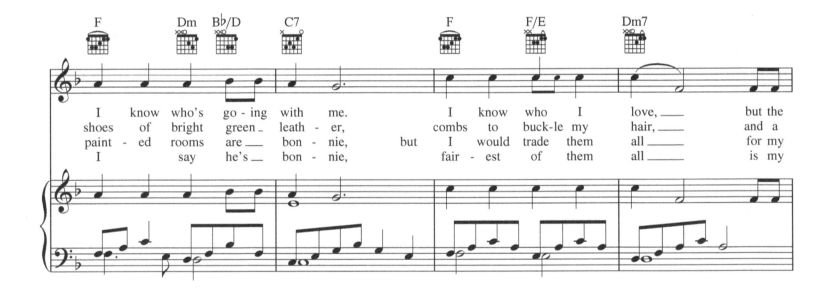

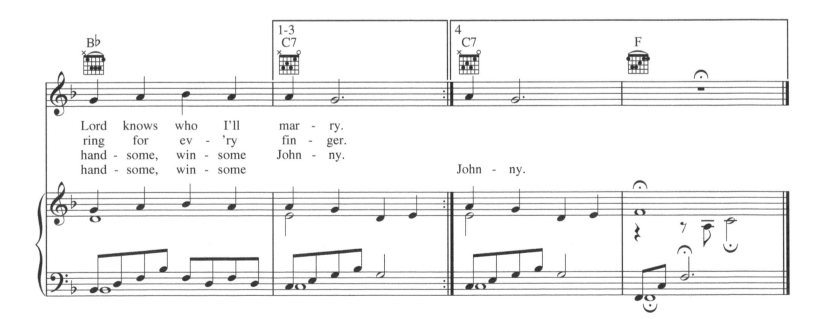

THE FOGGY DEW

Traditional Irish Folk Song

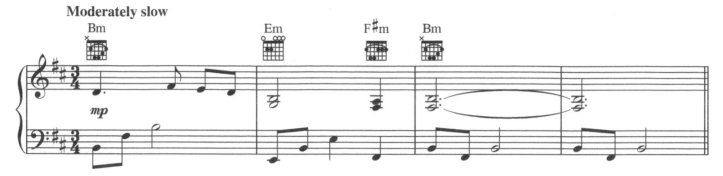

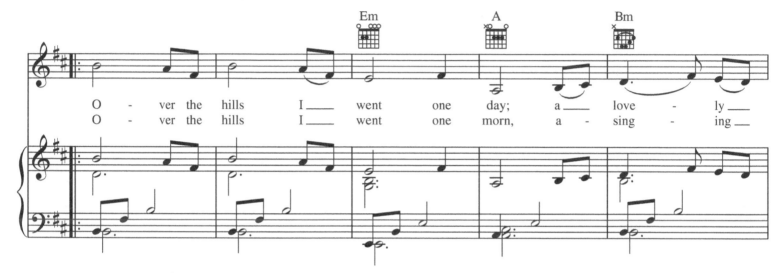

O - ver the hills I ___ went one day; a ___ love - ly ___
O - ver the hills I ___ went one morn, a sing - ing ___

maid I spied. _____ With her coal - black ___ hair and her
I did go. _____ Met this love - ly ___ maid with her

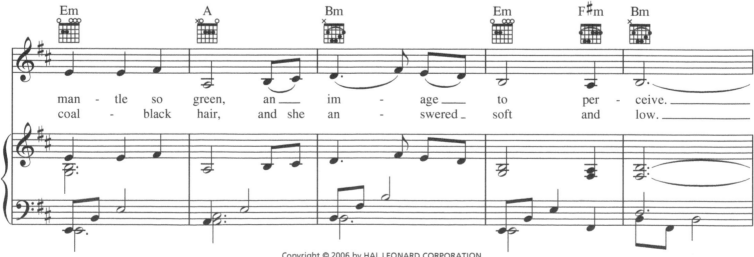

man - tle so green, an ___ im - age ___ to per - ceive. ___
coal - black hair, and she an - swered ___ soft and low. ___

Says I, "Dear girl, will you be my ___ bride?" And she
Said she, "Young man, I'll ___ be your ___ bride, if I

lift - ed her eyes of ___ blue. _____ She smiled and ___
know ___ that you'll be ___ true." _____ Oh, in ___ my ___

said, "Young man, I'm to wed; I'm to meet him in the
arms, all ___ of to her charms were ___ cast - ed in the

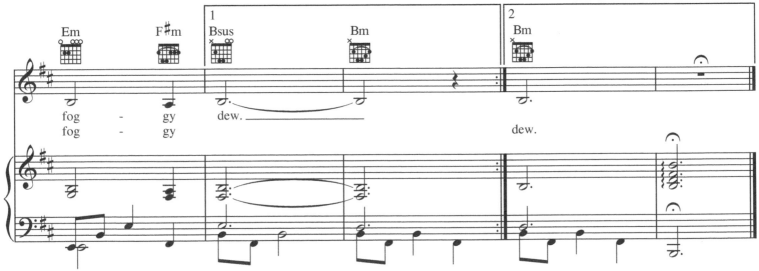

fog - gy dew. _____
fog - gy dew.

GREEN GROW THE RASHES, O

Traditional Irish Folk Song

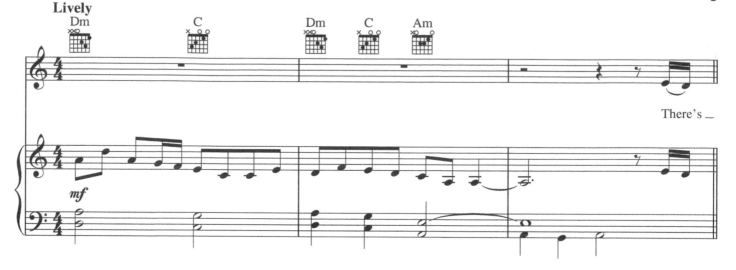

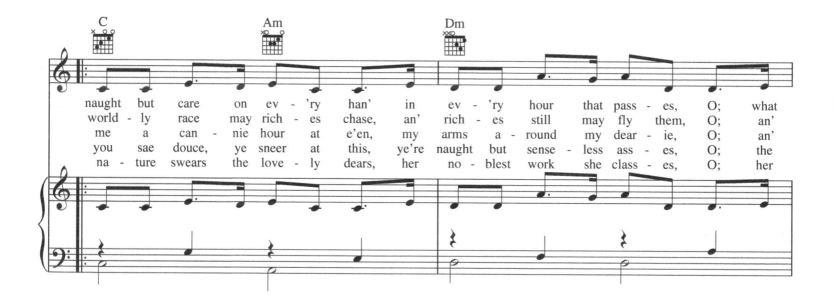

naught but care on ev-'ry han' in ev-'ry hour that pass-es, O; what
world - ly race may rich - es chase, an' rich - es still may fly them, O; an'
me a can - nie hour at e'en, my arms a - round my dear - ie, O; an'
you sae douce, ye sneer at this, ye're naught but sense - less ass - es, O; the
na - ture swears the love - ly dears, her no - blest work she class - es, O; her

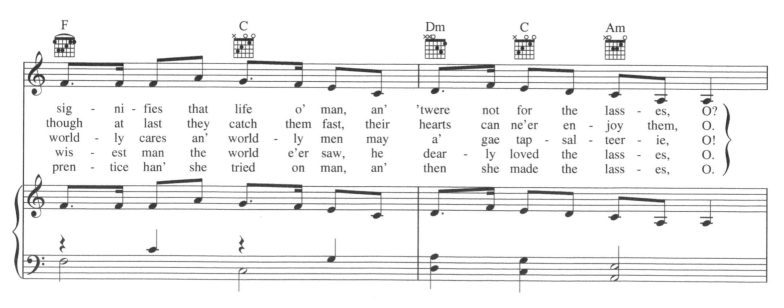

sig - ni - fies that life o' man, an' 'twere not for the lass - es, O?
though at last they catch them fast, their hearts can ne'er en - joy them, O.
world - ly cares an' world - ly men may a' gae tap - sal - teer - ie, O!
wis - est man the world e'er saw, he dear - ly loved the lass - es, O.
pren - tice han' she tried on man, an' then she made the lass - es, O.

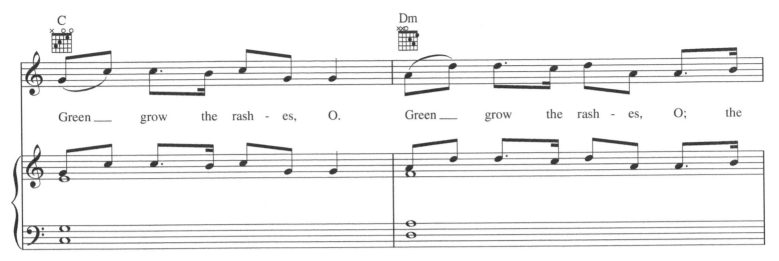

Green ___ grow the rash - es, O. Green ___ grow the rash - es, O; the

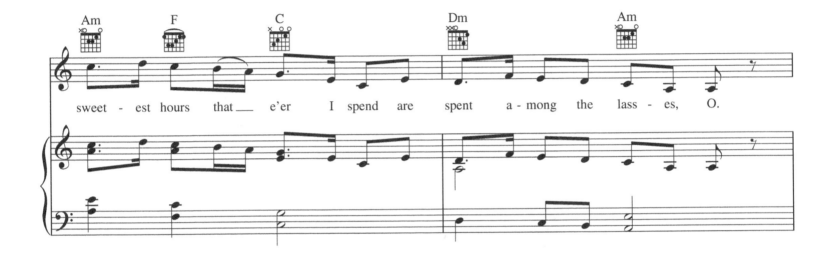

sweet - est hours that ___ e'er I spend are spent a - mong the lass - es, O.

The ___
Gie ___
An' ___
Auld ___

HENRY MY SON

Traditional Irish Folk Song

1. Where have you been all day, Hen - ry my son?
2. What did you have to eat, Hen - ry my son?
3. What col - our were those beads, Hen - ry my son?
4.-6. *(See additional lyrics)*

Where have you been all day, my be - lov - ed one? A -
What did you have to eat, my be - lov - ed one?
What col - our were those beads, my be - lov - ed one?

way in the mead - ow, a - way in the mead - ow.
Poi - son beads, poi - son beads.
Green and yel - low, green and yel - low.

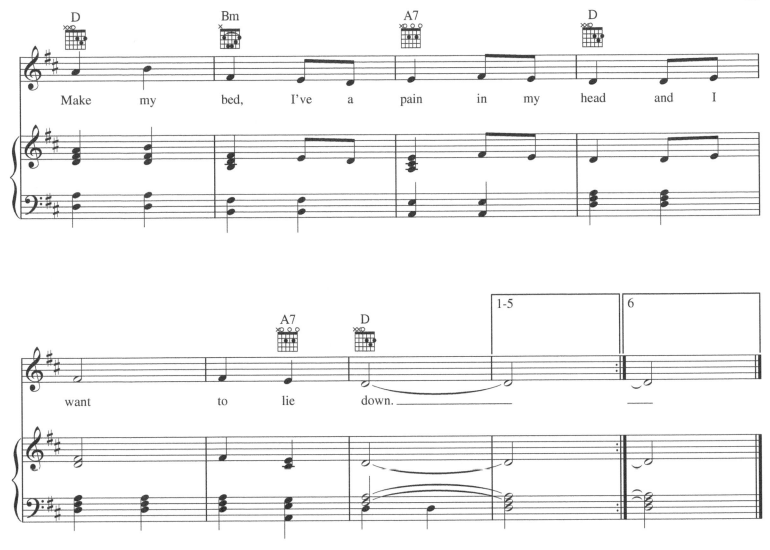

Additional Lyrics

4. What will you leave your mother, Henry my son?
   What will you leave your mother, my beloved one?
   A woolen blanket, a woolen blanket.
   Make my bed, I've a pain in my head and I want to lie down.

5. What will you leave your children, Henry my son?
   What will you leave your children, my beloved one?
   The keys of heaven, the keys of heaven.
   Make my bed, I've a pain in my head and I want to lie down.

6. And what will you leave your sweetheart, Henry my son?
   What will you leave your sweetheart, my beloved one?
   A rope to hang her, a rope to hang her.
   Make my bed, I've a pain in my head and I want to lie down.

I KNOW MY LOVE

Traditional Irish Folk Song

Moderately

I know my love by his way o' walk-in' and I
There is a dance house in Mar-a-dyke, ___ and there
If my love know I could wash and wring, ___ if ___
I know my love is an ar-rant rov-er, I ___

know my love by his way o' talk-in'. And I know my love in a
my true love goes ___ ev-'ry night. ___ He ___ takes a strange one up-
my love knew I could weave and spin, ___ I'd ___ make a coat of all the
know he'll wan-der the wild world o-ver. In ___ for-eign parts he may

suit of blue, and if my love leaves me, what will I do? ____
on his knee, and ____ don't you know, now, that vex - es me? ____
fin - est kind, but the love of mon - ey leaves me be - hind. ____
chance to stray, where ____ all the girls are so bright and gay. ____

And

still she cried, "I love him the best, and a trou - bled mind, sure, can

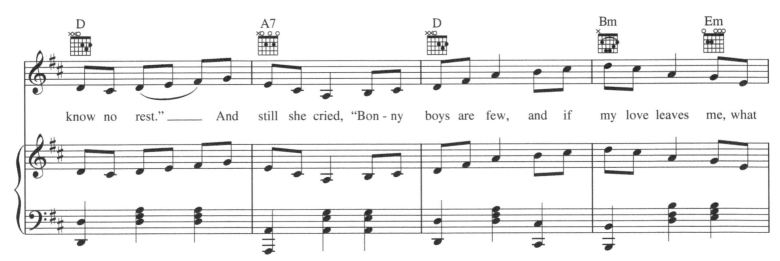

know no rest." ____ And still she cried, "Bon - ny boys are few, and if my love leaves me, what

will I do?" will I do?"

I NEVER WILL MARRY

Traditional Folk Song

1. I nev - er will mar - ry, I'll be no man's wife. I in - tend to stay sin -
2. day as I ram - bled down by the sea - shore, the wind it did whis -
3. heard a poor maid - en make a pit - i - ful cry. She sound - ed so lone -

4.,5. (See additional lyrics)

Additional Lyrics

4. "My love's gone and left me, he's the one I adore.
   I never will see him, no never, no more."

5. "The shells in the ocean will be my deathbed,
   And the fish in the water swim over my head."

6. She plunged her fair body in the water so deep.
   And she closed her pretty blue eyes in the water to sleep.

I'LL TELL ME MA

Traditional Irish Folk Song

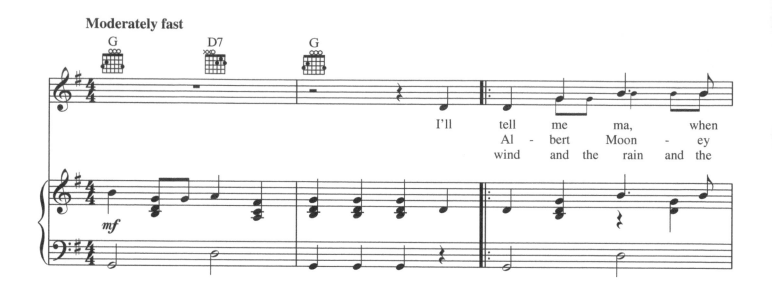

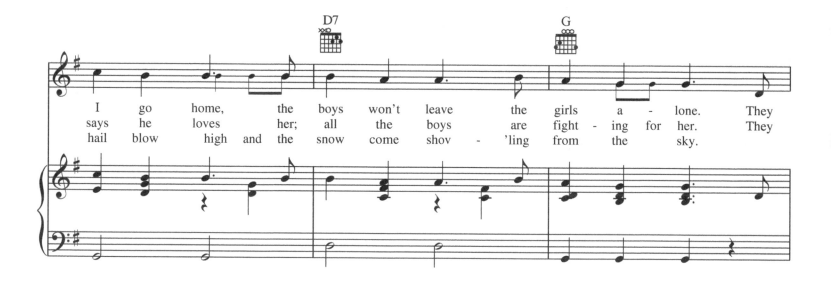

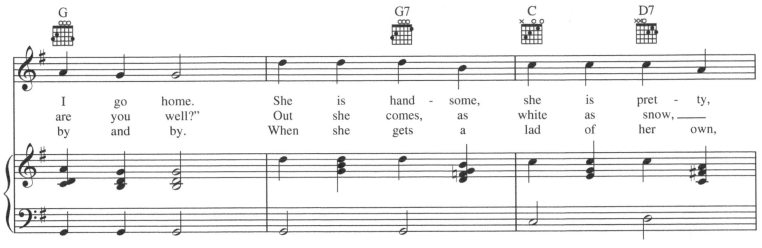

I go home. She is hand - some, she is pret - ty,
are you and well?" Out she comes, as white as snow, ___
by and by. When she gets a lad of her own,

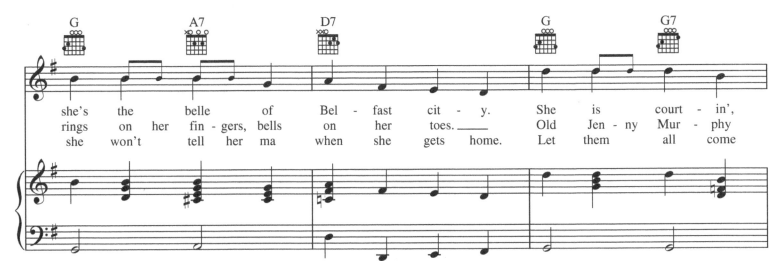

she's the belle of Bel - fast cit - y. She is court - in',
rings on her fin - gers, bells on her toes. ___ Old Jen - ny Mur - phy
she won't tell her ma on when she gets home. Let them all come

one, two, three. Please won't you tell me
says she'll die, but it's Al - bert Moon - ey
as they will, if she does - n't get the fel - low

who is she? Now she loves still.
with the rov - ing eye. Let the

I'M A ROVER AND SELDOM SOBER

Traditional Irish Folk Song

Additional Lyrics

4. "It's only me, your ain true lover;
   Open the door and let me in,
   For I hae come on a lang journey
   And I'm near drenched to the skin."
   Chorus

5. She opened the door wi' the greatest pleasure,
   She opened the door and she let him in;
   They baith shook hands and embraced each other,
   Until the mornin' they lay as one.
   Chorus

6. The cocks were crawin', the birds were whistlin',
   The burns they ran free abune the brae;
   "Remember, lass, I'm a ploughman laddie
   And the fairmer I must obey."
   Chorus

7. "Noo, my lass, I must gang and leave thee,
   And though the hills they are high above,
   I will climb them wi' greater pleasure
   Since I been in the airms o' my love."
   Chorus

JOHNNY I HARDLY KNEW YE

Traditional Irish Folk Song

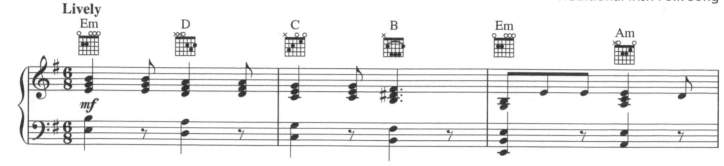

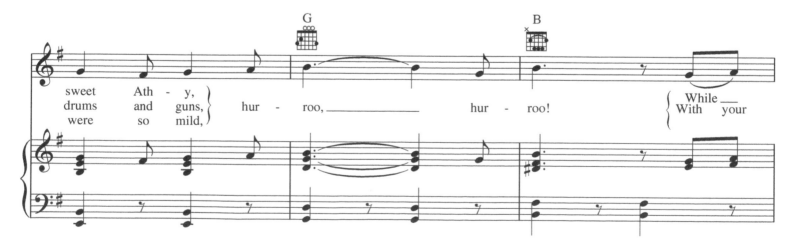

Additional Lyrics

4. Where are your legs that used to run, hurroo, hurroo!
Where are your legs that used to run, hurroo, hurroo!
Where are your legs that used to run
When you went for to carry a gun?
Indeed your dancing days are done.
Johnny I hardly knew ye.

5. I'm happy for to see you home, hurroo, hurroo!
I'm happy for to see you home, hurroo, hurroo!
I'm happy for to see you home
All from the island of Sulloon,
So low in flesh, so high in bone.
Johnny I hardly knew ye.

6. Ye haven't an arm, ye haven't a leg, hurroo, hurroo!
Ye haven't an arm, ye haven't a leg, hurroo, hurroo!
Ye haven't an arm, ye haven't a leg,
Ye're an armless, boneless, chickenless egg,
Ye'll have to put with a bowl out to beg.
Johnny I hardly knew ye.`

JUG OF PUNCH

Ulster Folk Song

'Twas ver - y

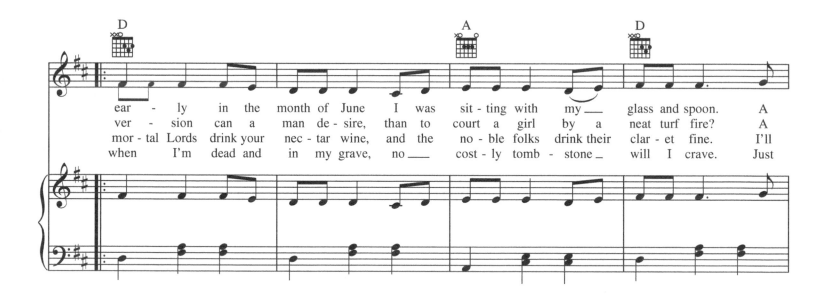

ear - ly in the month of June I was sit - ting with my __ glass and spoon. A
ver - sion can a man de - sire, than to court a girl by a neat turf fire? A
mor - tal Lords drink your nec - tar wine, and the no - ble folks drink their clar - et fine. I'll
when I'm dead and in my grave, no __ cost - ly tomb - stone __ will I crave. Just

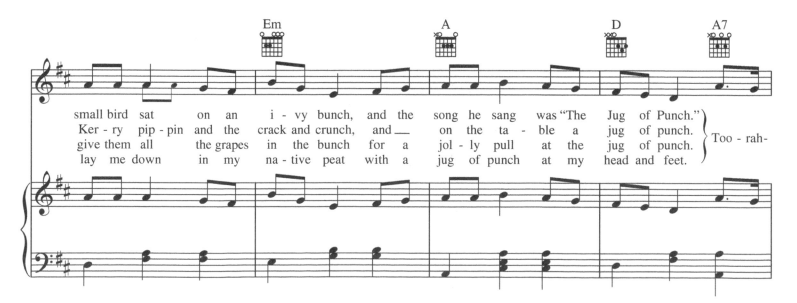

small bird sat on an i - vy bunch, and the song he sang was "The Jug of Punch."
Ker - ry pip - pin and the crack and crunch, and __ on the ta - ble a jug of punch.
give them all the grapes in the bunch for a jol - ly pull at the jug of punch.
lay me down in my na - tive peat with a jug of punch at my head and feet.

Too - rah-

loo - rah - loo, too - rah - loo - rah lay. Too - rah - loo - rah - loo, too - rah - loo - rah lay.

{ A
A
I'll
Just

small bird sat on an i - vy bunch, and the song he sang was "The
Ker - ry pip - pin and the crack and crunch, and on the ta - ble a
give them all the grapes in the bunch for a jol - ly pull at the
lay me down in my na - tive peat with a jug of punch at my

1–3
4

Jug of Punch."   What more di - head and feet.
jug of punch.   All ye
jug of punch.   Oh, but

LARK IN THE MORNING

Traditional Irish Folk Song

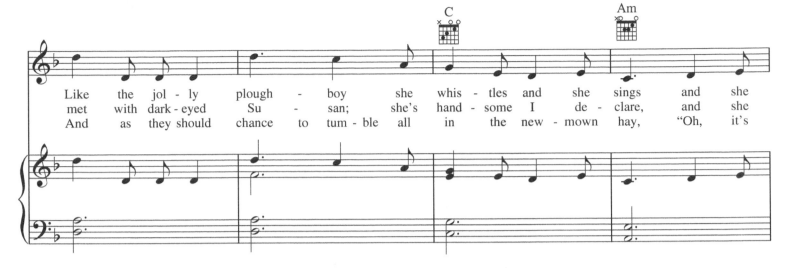

Like the jol - ly plough - boy she whis - tles and she sings and she
met with dark - eyed Su - san; she's hand - some I de - clare, and she
And as they should chance to tum - ble all in the new - mown hay, "Oh, it's

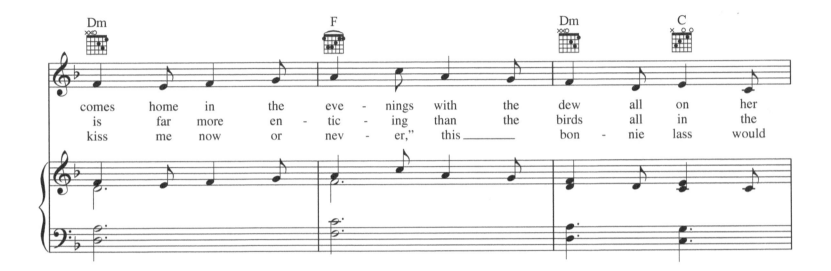

comes home in the eve - nings with the dew all on her
is far more en - tic - ing than the dew birds all in the
kiss me now or nev - er," this _____ bon - nie lass would

wings. _____
air. _____
say. _____

Oh,
As
When

Additional Lyrics

4. When twenty long weeks were over and had passed,
   Her mammy asked the reason why she thickened 'round the waist.
   "It was the pretty ploughboy," this lassie then did say,
   "For he asked me for to tumble all in the new-mown hay."

5. Here's a health to you ploughboys wherever you may be
   That like to have a bonnie lass a-sitting on each knee.
   With a pint of good strong porter he'll whistle and he'll sing,
   And the ploughboy is as happy as a prince or as a king.

'TIS THE LAST ROSE OF SUMMER

Words by THOMAS MOORE
Music by RICHARD ALFRED MILLIKEN

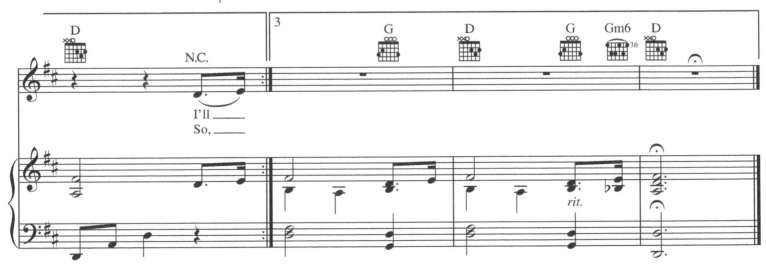

LEAVING OF LIVERPOOL

Irish Sea Chantey

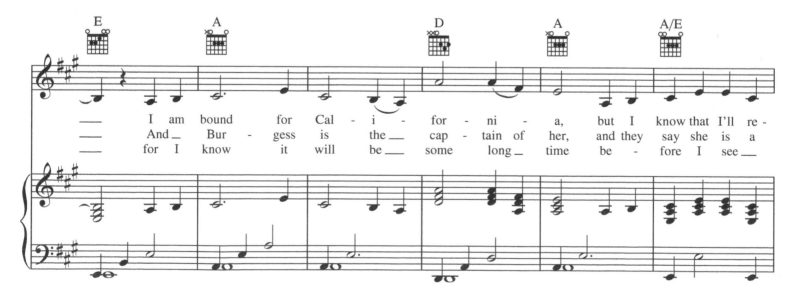

turn some day.
float - ing hell.
you a - gain.

So __ fare thee well, my __ own true

love, and when I re - turn, u - nit - ed we will be. It's not the

leav - ing of Liv - er - pool that grieves _____ me, but my

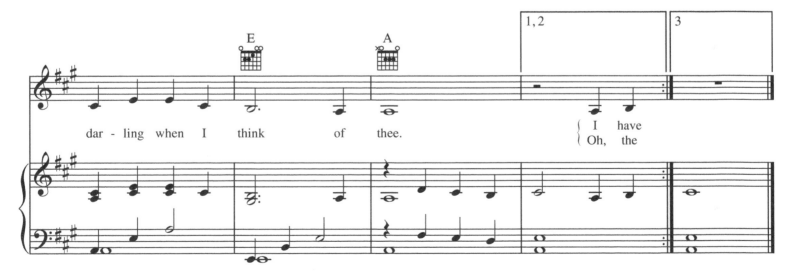

dar - ling when I think of thee.

I have
Oh, the

THE MEETING OF THE WATERS

Traditional Irish Folk Song

THE MERMAID

18th Century Sea Chantey

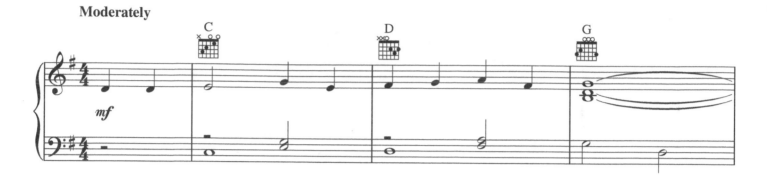

1. It was Fri - day morn when we ____ set ____
2. spoke the cap - tain of our gal - lant
3. spoke the mate of our gal - lant
4.-6. *(See additional lyrics)*

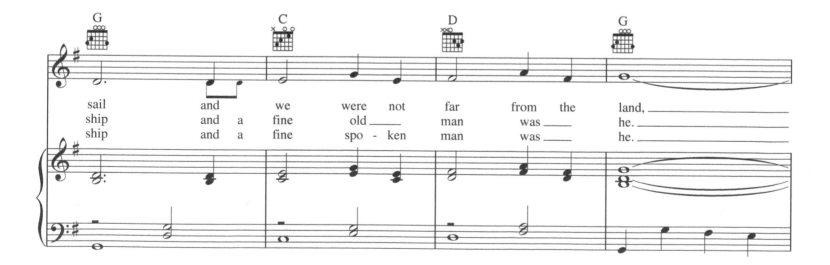

sail ____ and we were not far from the land, ____
ship and a fine old ____ man was ____ he. ____
ship and a fine spo - ken man was ____ he. ____

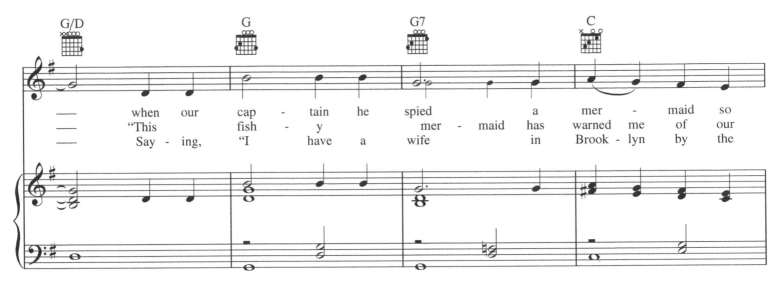

when our cap - tain he spied a mer - maid so
"This fish - y mer - maid has warned me of our
Say - ing, "I have a wife in Brook - lyn by the

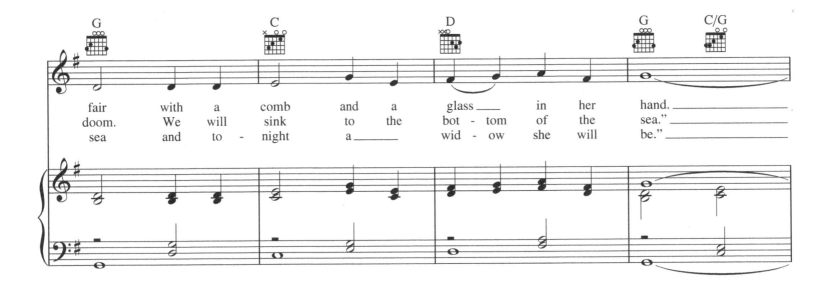

fair with a comb and a glass___ in her hand.___
doom. We will sink to the bot - tom of her sea."___
sea and to - night a___ wid - ow she will be."___

Refrain

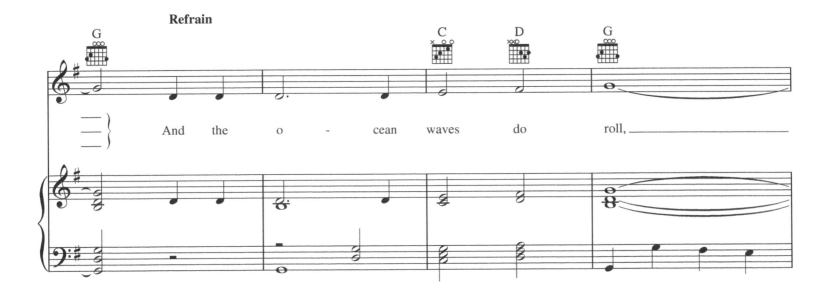

And the o - cean waves do roll,___

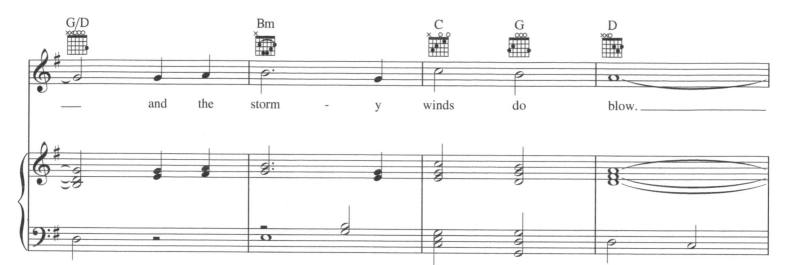

and the storm - y winds do blow.

And we poor sail - ors are skip - ping at the

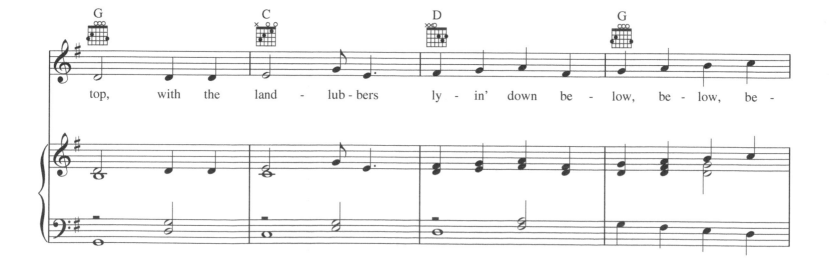

top, with the land - lub - bers ly - in' down be - low, be - low, be -

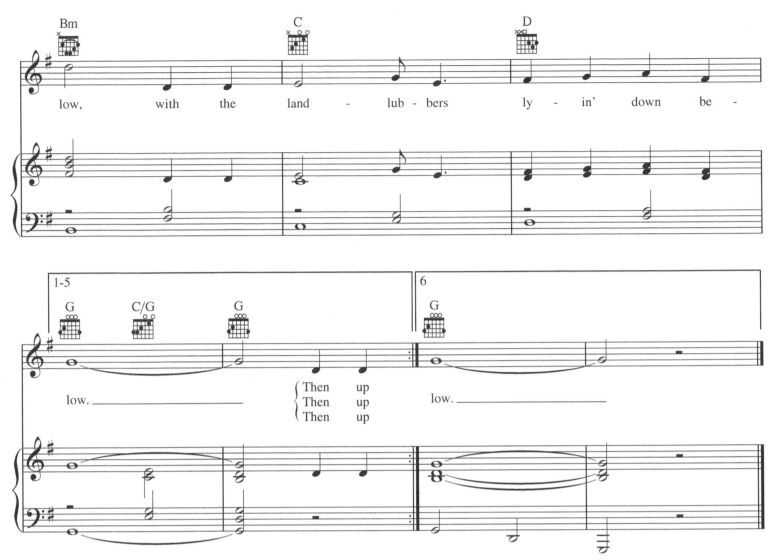

low, with the land - lub - bers ly - in' down be -

1-5
G   C/G   G
low. _____

Then up
Then up
Then up

6
G
low. _____

Additional Lyrics

4. Then up spoke the cabin boy of our gallant ship and a brave young lad was he.
   "I have a sweetheart in Salem by the sea and tonight she'll be weeping for me."
   Refrain

5. Then up spoke the cook of our gallant ship and a crazy old butcher was he.
   "I care so much more for my skillets and my pans than I do for the bottom of the sea."
   Refrain

6. Then three times around spun our gallant ship and three times around spun she.
   Three times around spun our gallant ship and she sank to the bottom of the sea.
   Refrain

MINSTREL BOY

Traditional

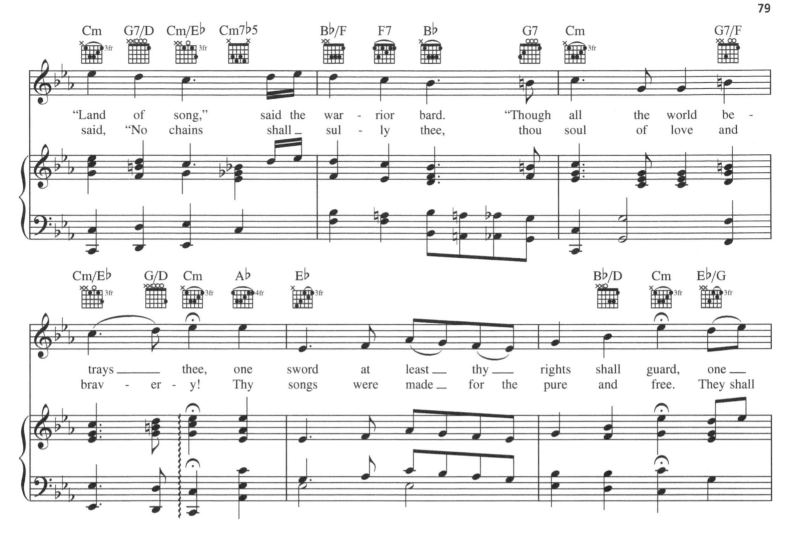

"Land of song," said the war - rior bard. "Though all the world be -
said, "No chains shall __ sul - ly thee, thou soul of love and

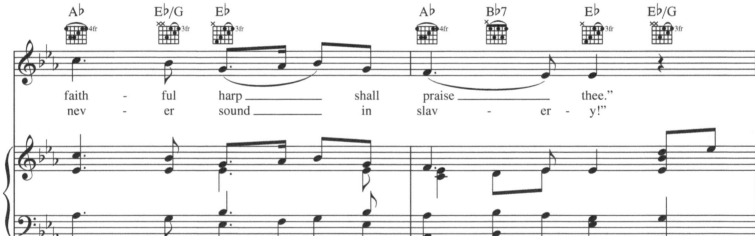

trays __ thee, one sword at least __ thy __ rights shall guard, one __
brav - er - y! Thy songs were made __ for the pure and free. They shall

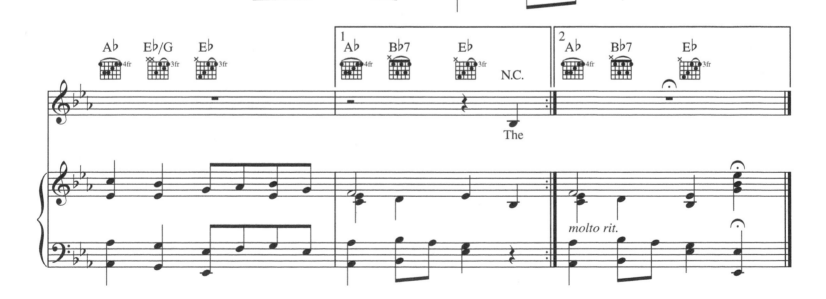

faith - ful harp _____ shall praise _____ thee."
nev - er sound _____ in slav - er - y!"

The

molto rit.

MOLLY MALONE
(Cockles & Mussels)

Irish Folk Song

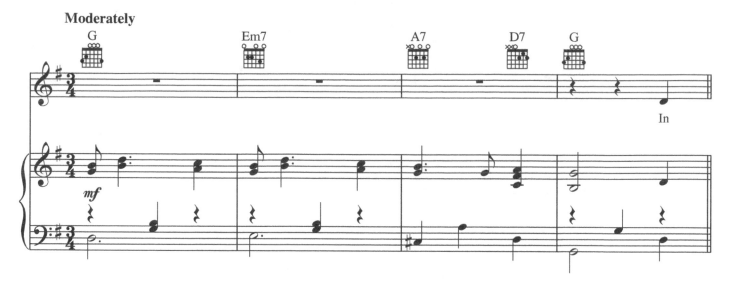

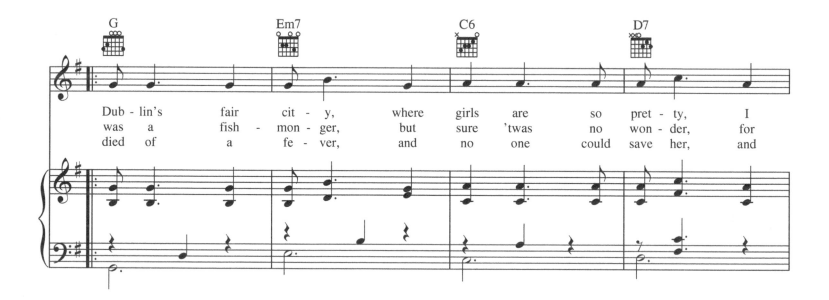

Dub - lin's fair cit - y, where girls are so pret - ty, I
was a fish - mon - ger, but sure 'twas no won - der, I for
died of a fe - ver, and sure no one could save her, and

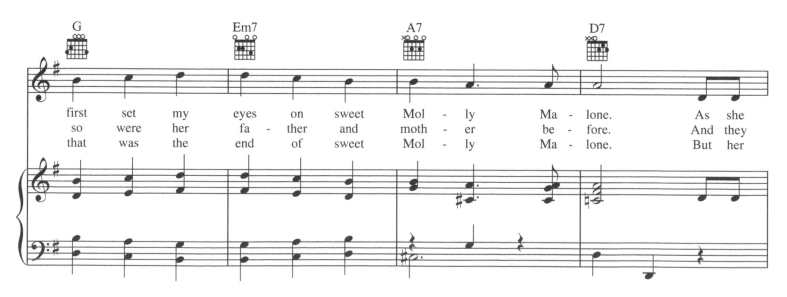

first set my eyes on sweet Mol - ly Ma - lone. As she
so were her fa - ther and moth - er be - fore. And they
that was the end of sweet Mol - ly Ma - lone. But her

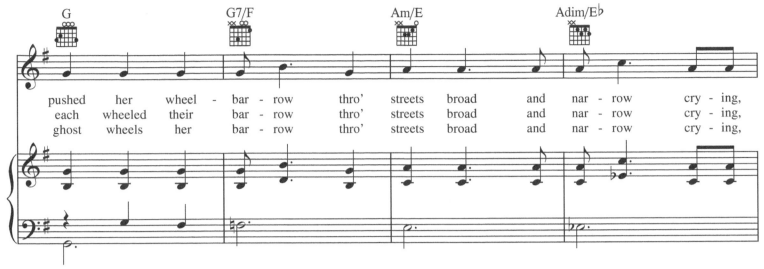

pushed her wheel - bar - row thro' streets broad and nar - row cry - ing,
each wheeled their bar - row thro' streets broad and nar - row cry - ing,
ghost wheels her bar - row thro' streets broad and nar - row cry - ing,

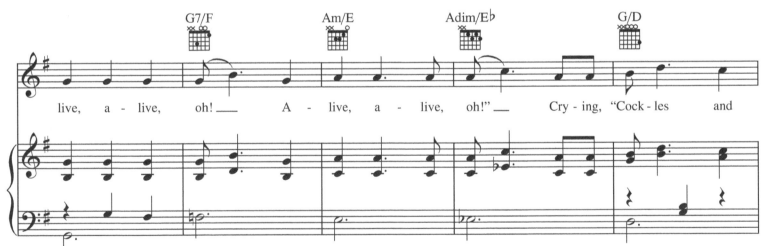

"Cock - les and mus - sels, a - live, a - live, oh!
"Cock - les and mus - sels, a - live, a - live, oh! A -
"Cock - les and mus - sels, a - live, a - live, oh!

live, a - live, oh! __ A - live, a - live, oh!" __ Cry - ing, "Cock - les and

mus - sels, a - live, a - live, oh!" { She
                                      { She   oh!"

THE MOUNTAINS OF MOURNE

Words by PERCY FRENCH
Traditional Irish Melody

MY SINGING BIRD

Traditional

Moderately

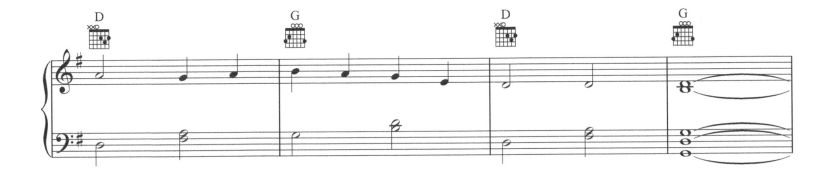

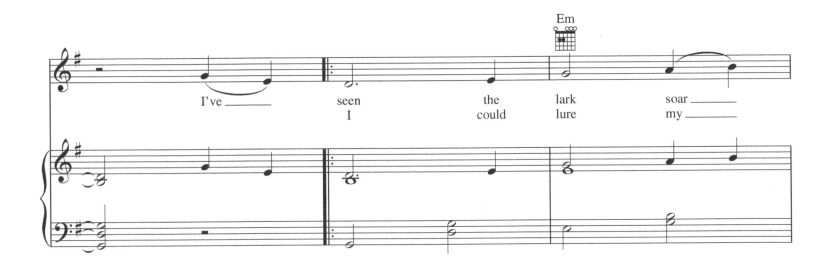

I've _____ seen the lark soar _____
I could lure my _____

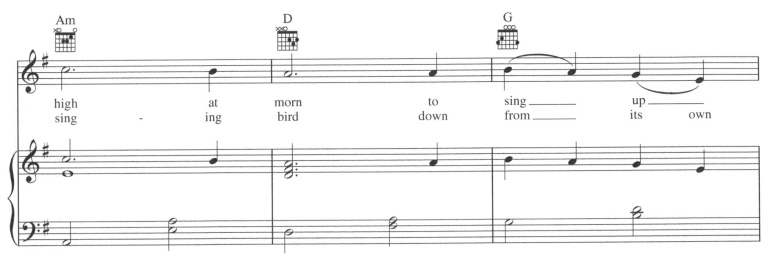

high _____ at morn to sing _____ up _____
sing - ing bird to down from _____ its _____ own

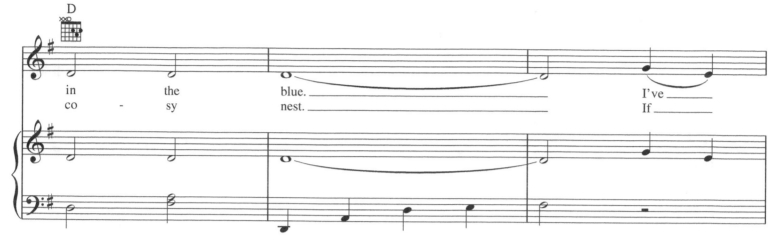

sing so sweet, my sing - ing bird _____ as _____
sing - ing sweet bird my would sing it - self _____ to _____

you. _____ Ah, ah, ah, ah, ah, ah, ah,
rest. _____

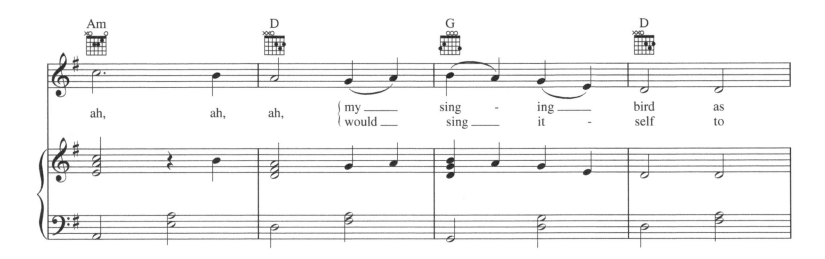

ah, ah, ah, my _____ sing - ing _____ bird as _____
would _____ sing _____ it - self _____ to

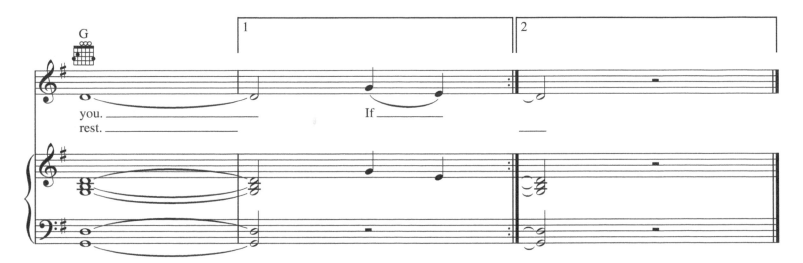

you. _____ If _____
rest. _____

A NATION ONCE AGAIN

Words and Music by
THOMAS DAVIS

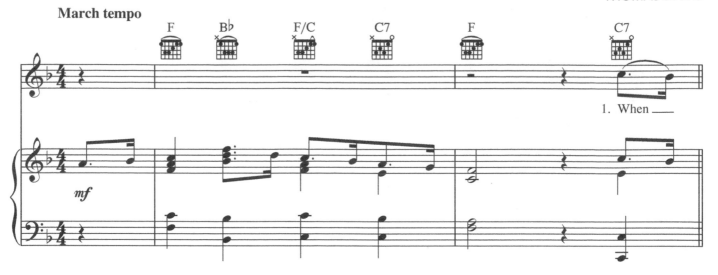

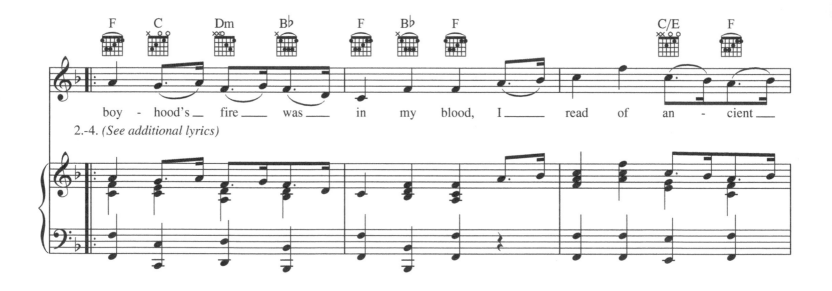

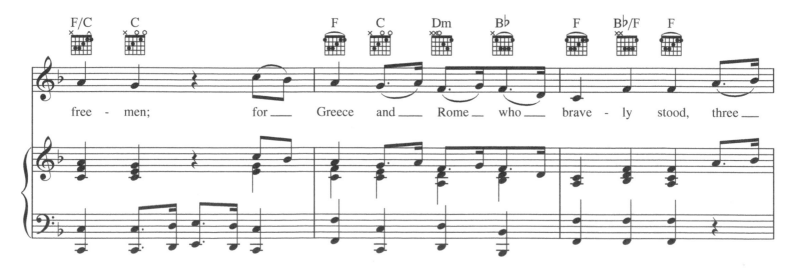

hun - dred ___ men ___ and ___ three men. And there I prayed I

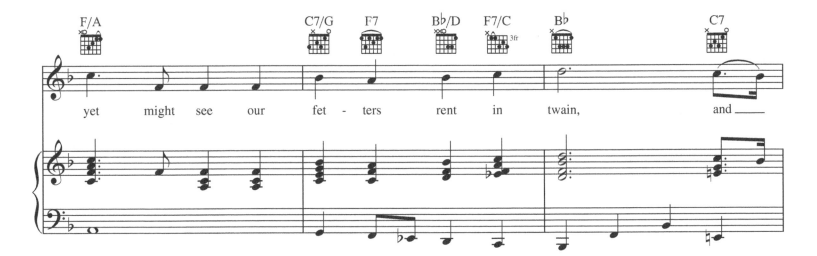

yet might see our fet - ters rent in twain, and ___

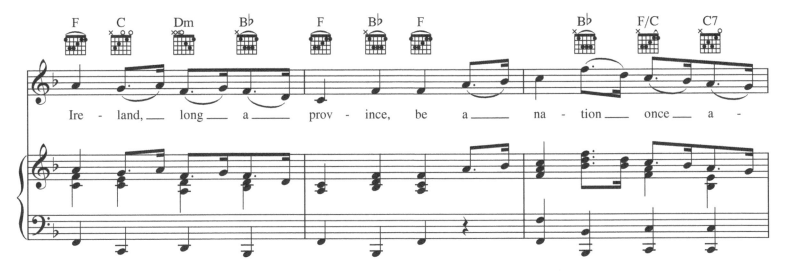

Ire - land, ___ long ___ a ___ prov - ince, be a ___ na - tion ___ once a -

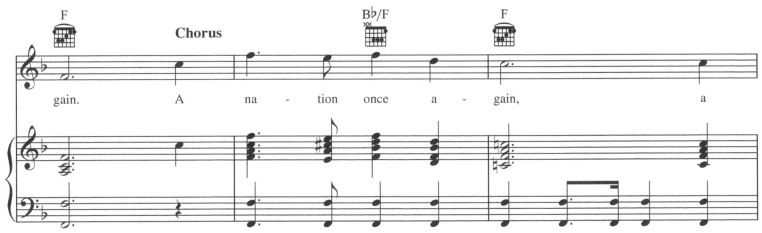

gain. A na - tion once a - gain, a

na - tion once a - gain. May Ire - land, long a

prov - ince, be a na - tion once a - gain. And from gain?

Additional Lyrics

2. And from that time, through wildest woe,
That hope has shown a far light;
Nor could love's brightest summer glow
Outshine that solemn starlight.
It seemed to watch above my head
In forum, field and fane;
Its angel voice sang 'round my bed,
"A nation once again."
Chorus

3. It whispered too, that "Freedom's Ark"
And service high and holy,
Would be profaned by feelings dark
And passions vain or lowly;
For freedom comes from God's right hand,
And needs a Godly train,
And righteous men must make our land
A nation once again.
Chorus

4. So as I grew from boy to man,
I bent me at that bidding;
My spirit of each selfish plan
And cruel passion ridding.
For thus I hoped some day to aid.
Oh! Can such hope be vain
When my dear country shall be made
A nation once again?
Chorus

THE PATRIOT GAME

Traditional Irish Folk Song

1. Come all you young reb - els and list while I sing. For
2. name is O' - Han - lon, I'm just gone six - teen. My
3. bare - ly two years since I wan - dered a - way with the

4.-8. (See additional lyrics)

Additional Lyrics

4. They told me how Connolly was shot in a chair.
   His wounds from the battle all bleeding and bare,
   His fine body twisted, all battered and lame.
   They soon made him part of the patriot game.

5. I joined a battalion from dear Bally Bay,
   And gave up my boyhood so happy and gay.
   For now as a soldier I'd drill and I'd train,
   To play my full part in the patriot game.

6. This Ireland of mine has for long been half free.
   Six counties are under John Bull's tyranny.
   And still De Valera is greatly to blame
   For shirking his part in the patriot game.

7. I don't mind a bit if I shoot down police.
   They're lackeys for war never guardians of peace.
   But yet at deserters I'm never let aim,
   Those rebels who sold out the patriot game.

8. And now as I lie with my body all holes
   I think of those traitors who bargained and sold.
   I'm sorry my rifle has not done the same
   For the quisling who sold out the patriot game.

O'DONNELL ABOO

Words and Music by
M.J. McCANN

March tempo

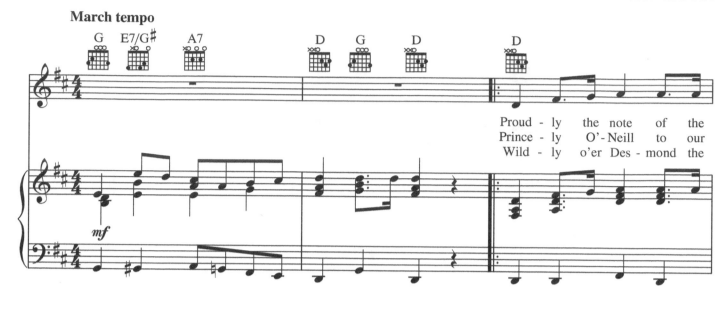

Proud - ly the note of the
Prince - ly O'- Neill to our
Wild - ly o'er Des - mond the

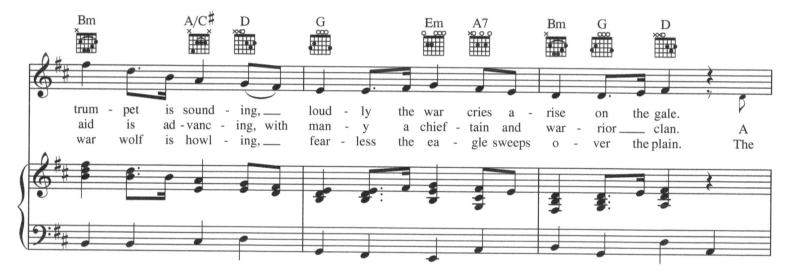

trum - pet is sound - ing, ___ loud - ly the war cries a - rise on the gale.
aid is ad - vanc - ing, with man - y a chief - tain and war - rior ___ clan.
war wolf is howl - ing, ___ fear - less the ea - gle sweeps o - ver the plain.

A
The

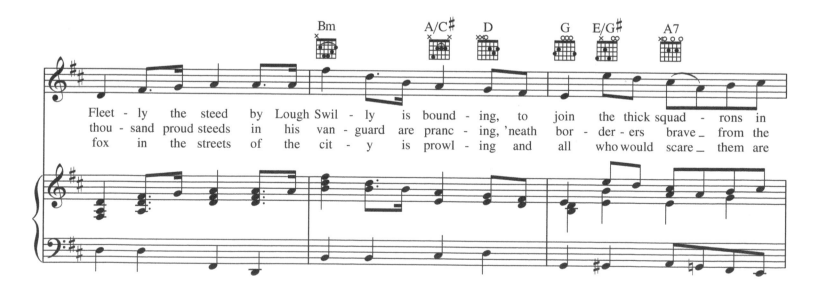

Fleet - ly the steed by Lough Swil - ly is bound - ing, to join the thick squad - rons in
thou - sand proud steeds in his van - guard are pranc - ing, 'neath bor - der - s brave ___ from the
fox in the streets of the cit - y is prowl - ing and all who would scare ___ them are

THE RAGGLE-TAGGLE GYPSY

Traditional

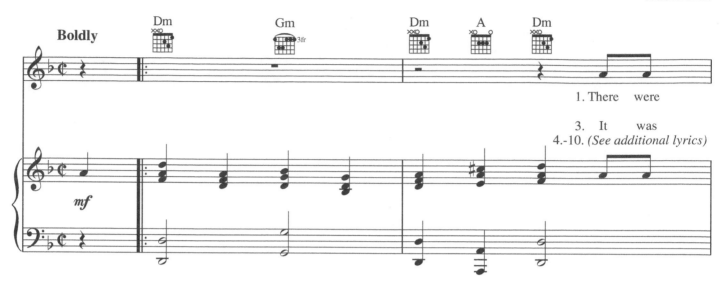

Boldly

1. There were
3. It was
4.-10. *(See additional lyrics)*

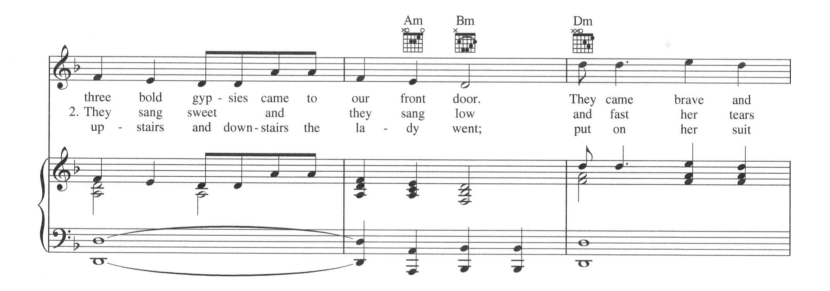

three bold gyp-sies came to our front door.
2. They sang sweet and they sang low
up-stairs and down-stairs the la-dy went;

They came brave and
and fast her tears
put on her suit

bold-ly - o and there's one sang high and the oth-er sang __ low. And the
be-gan to flow. She __ laid down her __ silk - en __ gown, her __
of leath-er-o. And it was the cry all a - round __ the __ door, "She's a -

Additional Lyrics

4. It was late that night when the lord came home inquiring for his lady-o.
   The servant's voice rang around the house, "She is gone with the raggle-taggle gypsy-o."

5. "Oh then saddle for me, my milk white steed; the black horse is not speedy-o.
   And I will ride and I'll seek me bride who's away with the raggle-taggle gypsy-o."

6. Oh then he rode high and he rode low; he rode north and south also,
   But when he came to a wide open field it is there that he spotted his lady-o.

7. "Oh then why did you leave your house and your land; why did you leave your money-o
   And why did you leave your newly wedded lord to be off with the raggle-taggle gypsy-o."

8. "Yerra what do I care for me house and me land and what do I care for money-o.
   And what do I care for my newly-wedded lord; I'm away with the raggle-taggle gypsy-o?"

9. "And what do I care for my goose-feathered bed with blankets drawn so comely-o.
   Tonight I'll sleep in the wide open field all along with the raggle-taggle gypsy-o."

10. "Oh for you rode east when I rode west; you rode high and I rode low,
    I'd rather have a kiss from the yellow gypsy's lips than all your land and money-o."

RED IS THE ROSE

Irish Folk Song

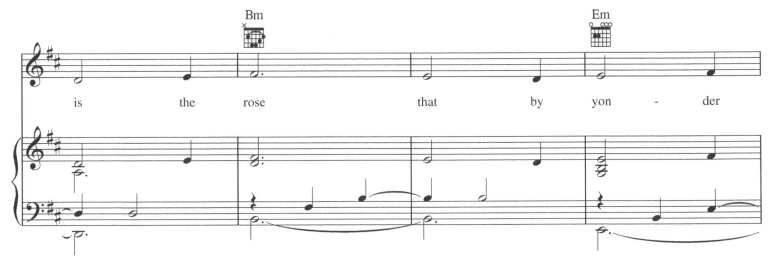

is the rose that by yon - der

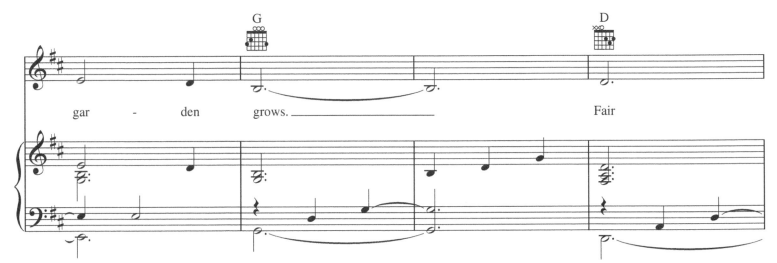

gar - den grows. _____ Fair

is the li - ly of the val -

- ley. _____ Clear

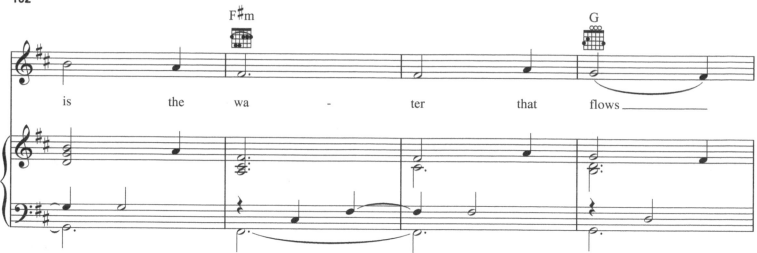

is the wa - ter that flows _____

from the Boyne. But _____ my

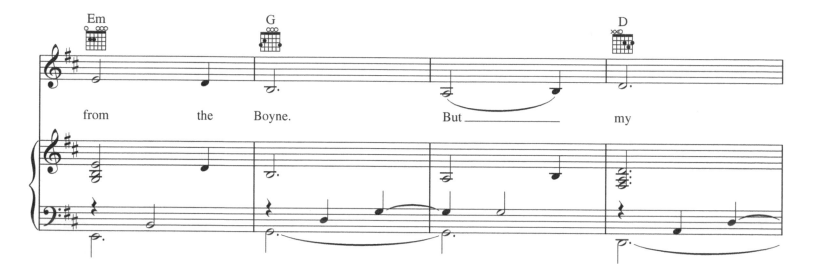

love is fair - er than an -

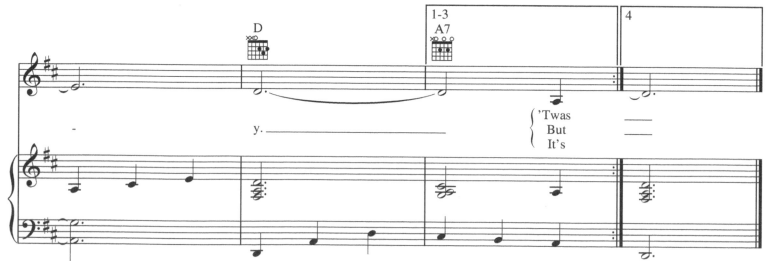

- y. _____

'Twas
But
It's

THE ROCKS OF BAWN

Traditional Irish Folk Song

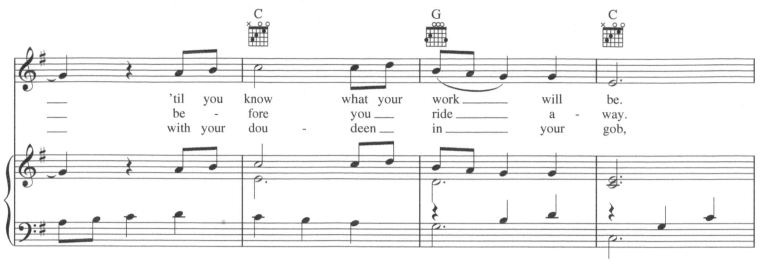

'til you know what your work ___ will be.
be - fore you ___ ride ___ a - way.
with your dou - deen ___ in ___ your gob,

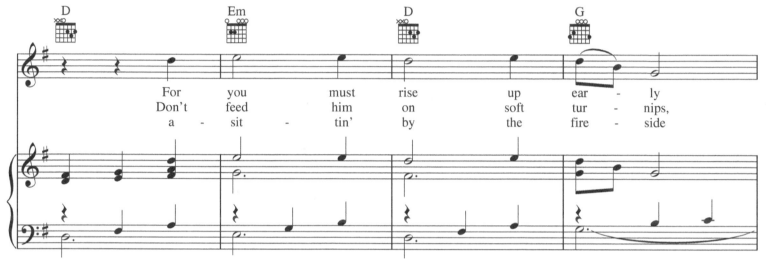

For you must rise up ear - ly
Don't feed him on soft tur - nips,
a - sit - tin' by the fire - side

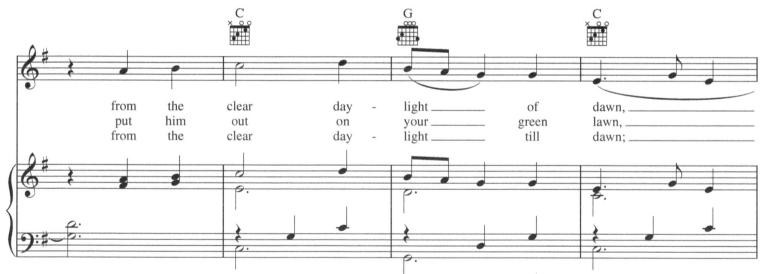

from the clear day - light ___ of dawn,
put him out on your ___ green lawn,
from the clear day - light ___ till dawn;

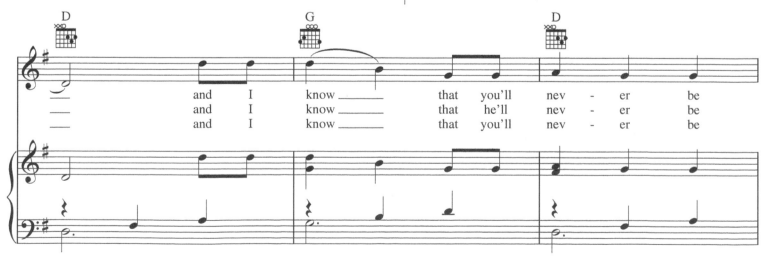

and I know ___ that you'll nev - er be
and I know ___ that he'll nev - er be
and I know ___ that you'll nev - er be

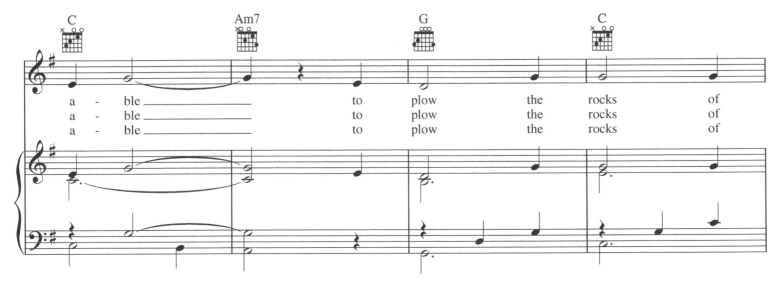

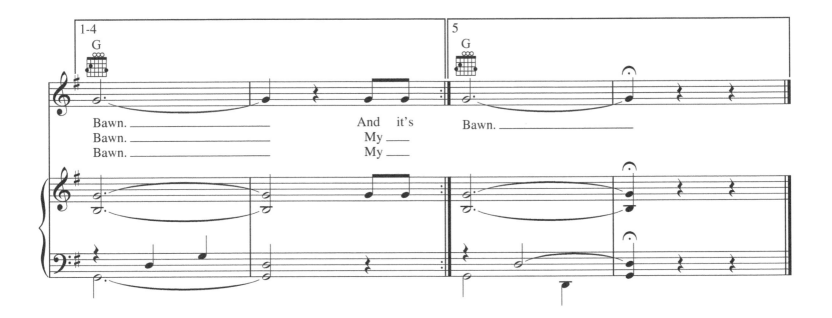

Additional Lyrics

4. My shoes they are well worn out, my stockings they are thin,
And my heart is always trembling for fear that they'll let in.
And my heart is always trembling from the clear daylight of dawn,
Afraid I'll never be able to plow the rocks of Bawn.

5. I wish the Queen of England would write to me in time
And place me in some regiment in all my youth and prime.
I'd fight for Ireland's glory from the clear daylight of dawn,
And I never would return again to plow the rocks of Bawn.

THE ROCKY ROAD TO DUBLIN

Traditional Irish Folk Song

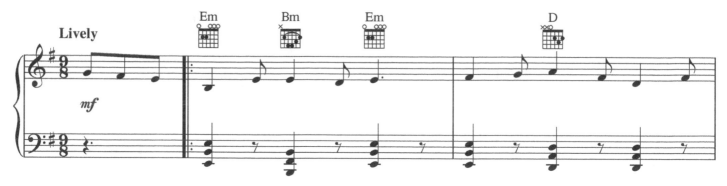

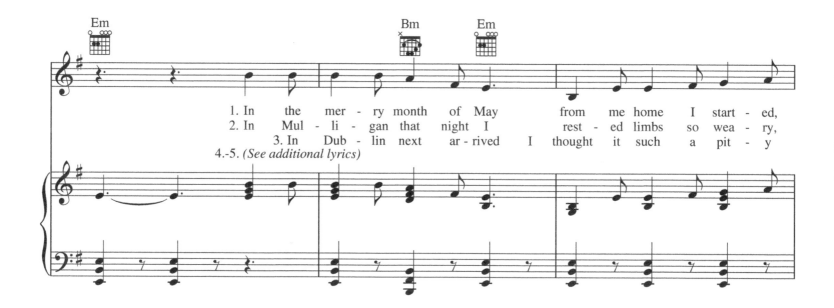

1. In the mer-ry month of May   from me home I start - ed,
2. In Mul-li - gan that night I   rest - ed limbs so wea - ry,
3. In Dub - lin next ar - rived I thought it such a pit - y
4.-5. *(See additional lyrics)*

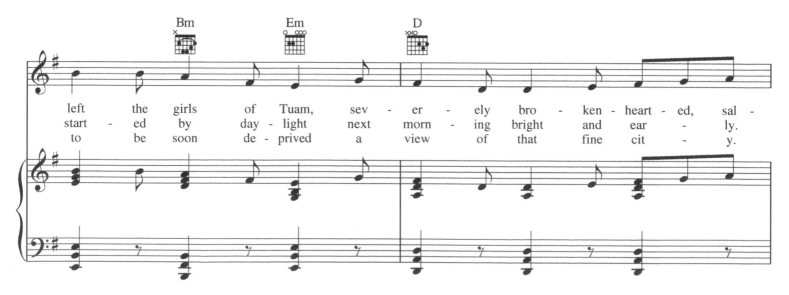

left the girls of Tuam, sev - er - ely bro - ken - heart - ed, sal -
start - ed by day - light next morn - ing bright and ear - ly.
to be soon de - prived a view of that fine cit - y.

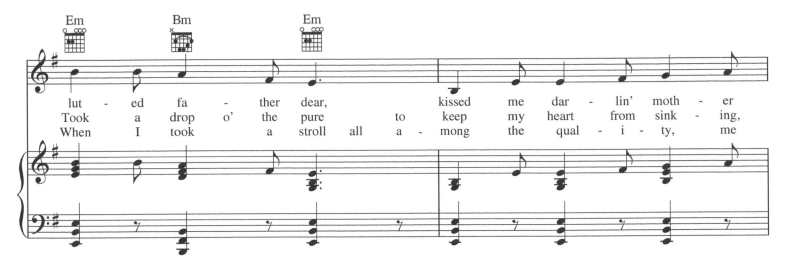

lut - ed fa - ther dear, kissed me dar - lin' moth - er
Took a drop o' the pure to keep my heart from sink - ing,
When I took a stroll all a - mong the qual - i - ty, me

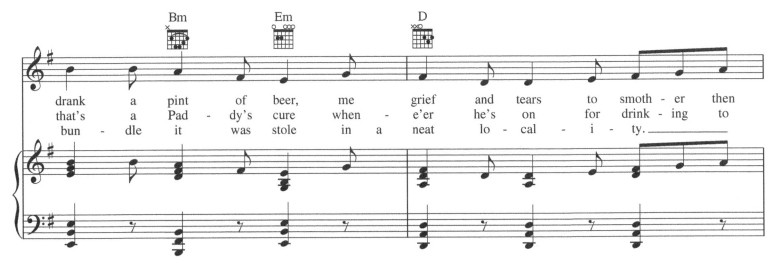

drank a pint of beer, me grief and tears to smoth - er then
that's a Pad - dy's cure when - e'er he's on for drink - ing to
bun - dle it was stole in a neat lo - cal - i - ty. _____

off to reap the corn, leave where I was born,
see the las - sie's smile, laugh - ing all the while,
Some - thing crossed me mind, then I looked be - hind, no

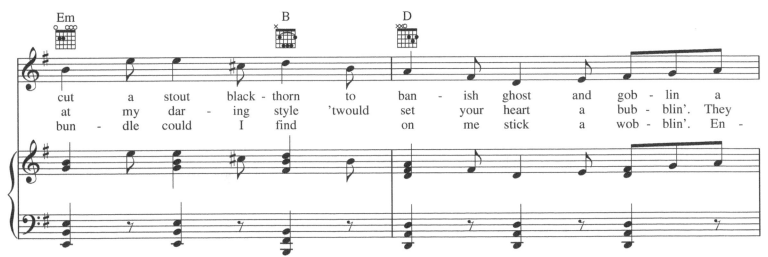

cut a stout black - thorn to ban - ish ghost and gob - lin a
at my dar - ing style 'twould set your heart a bub - blin'. They
bun - dle could I find on me stick a wob - blin'. En -

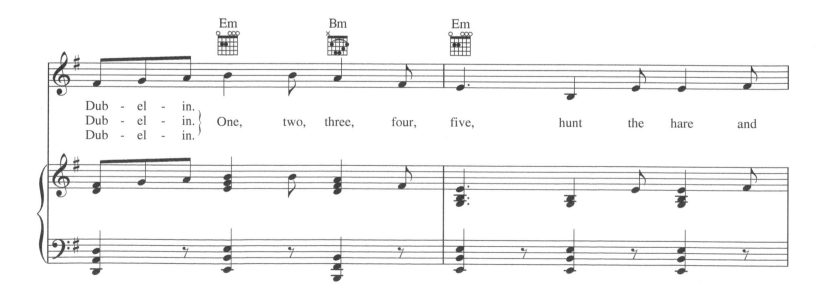

Additional Lyrics

4. From there I got away, me spirits never failing,
   Landed on the quay as the ship was sailing.
   Captain at me roared, said that no room had he.
   When I jumped aboard, a cabin for Paddy
   Down among the pigs I played some funny rigs
   Danced some hearty jigs, the water 'round me bubblin'
   When off Holyhead I wished meself was dead
   Or better far instead, on the rocky road to Dublin.

5. The boys of Liverpool when we safely landed
   Called meself a fool, I could no longer stand it.
   Blood began to boil, temper I was losing.
   Poor old Erin's Isle they began abusing.
   "Hurrah, me boys," says I, shillelagh I let fly
   Some Galway boys were by and saw I was a-hobblin'.
   Then with loud "Hurray!" they joined in the affray
   And quickly paved the way for the rocky road to Dublin.

RODDY McCORLEY

Traditional Irish Folk Song

Moderately

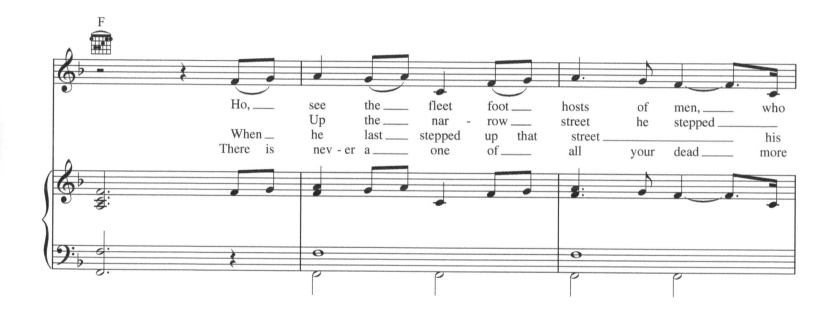

Ho, ___ see the ___ fleet foot ___ hosts of men, ___ who
Up the ___ nar - row ___ street he stepped ___
When ___ he last stepped up that street ___ his
There is nev - er a ___ one of all your dead ___ more

speed with fac - es wan, from ___ farm - stead and from ___
smil - ing and proud and young, a - bout the hemp - rope ___
shin - ing pike in hand, be - hind him marched in ___
brave - ly fell in fray, then ___ he who march - es ___

THE ROSE OF TRALEE

Words by C. MORDAUNT SPENCER
Music by CHARLES W. GLOVER

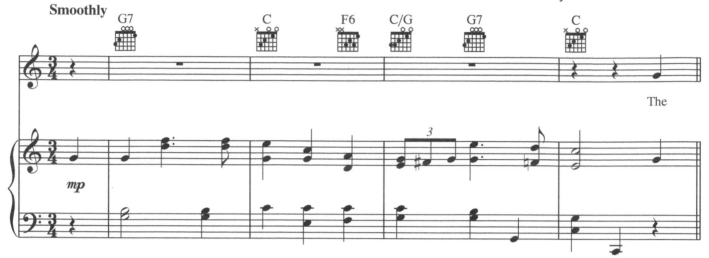

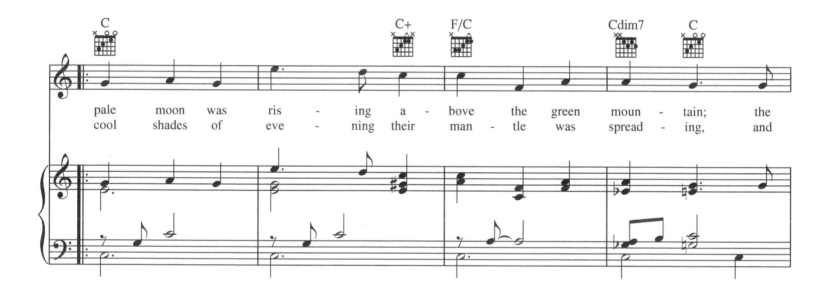

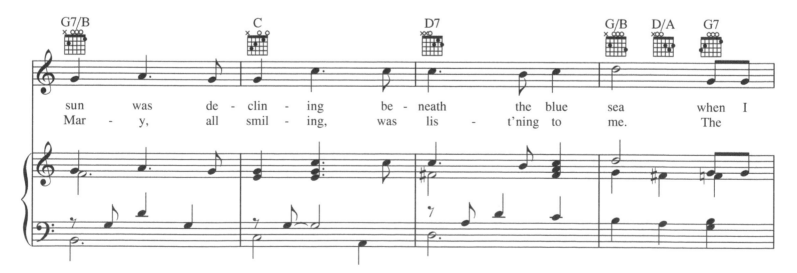

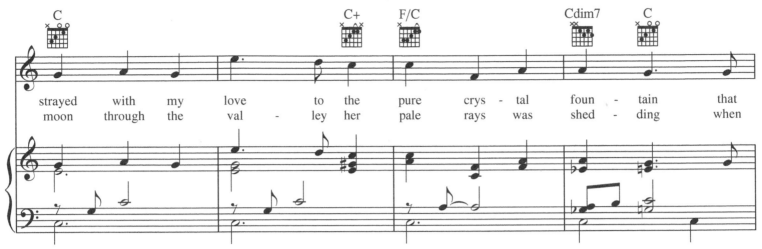

strayed with my love to the pure crys - tal foun - tain that
moon with through the val - ley her pale rays was shed - ding that when

stands in the beau - ti - ful vale of Tra -
I won the heart of the rose of Tra -

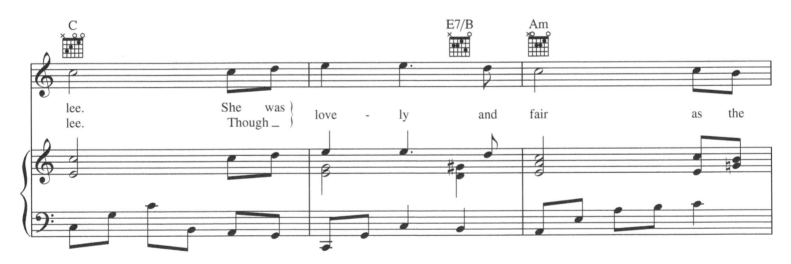

lee. She was
lee. Though love - ly and fair as the

rose of the sum - mer, yet 'twas not her

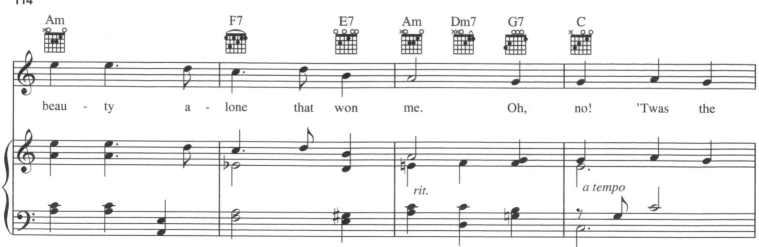

beau - ty a - lone that won me. Oh, no! 'Twas the

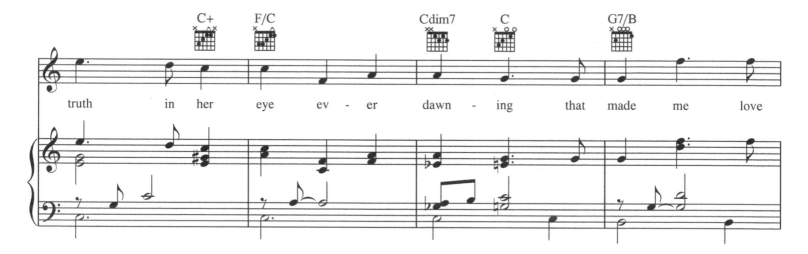

truth in her eye ev - er dawn - ing that made me love

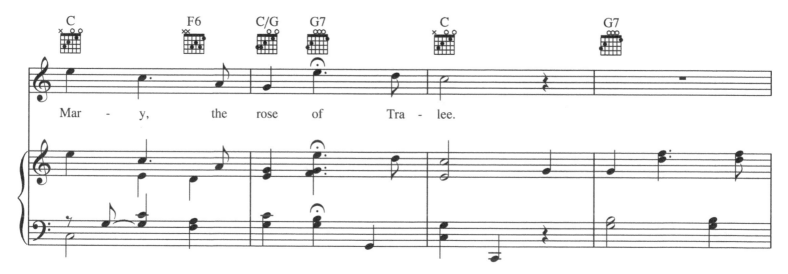

Mar - y, the rose of Tra - lee.

The

WHISKEY IN THE JAR

Traditional Irish Folk Song

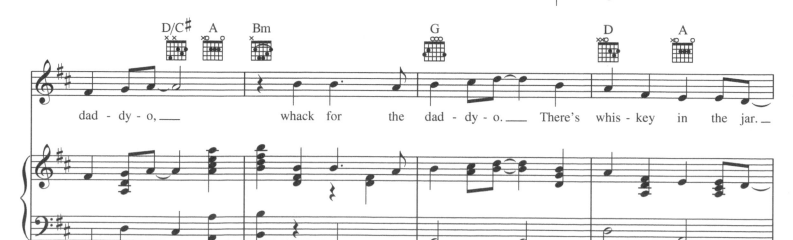

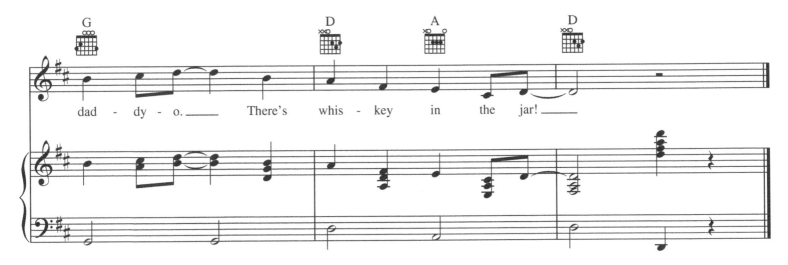

Additional Lyrics

4. Some take delight in the fishin' and the fowlin'.
   Others take delight in the carriage gently rollin'.
   Ah, but I take delight in the juice of the barley;
   Courtin' pretty women in the mountains of Killarney.
   Musha ring dumma doo-rama da.
   Chorus

ROSIN THE BOW

Traditional

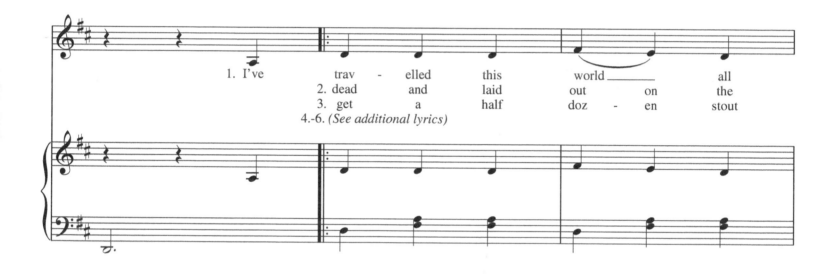

1. I've   trav - elled   this   world _____   all
2. dead   and   laid   out   on   the
3. get   a   half   doz - en   stout
4.-6. *(See additional lyrics)*

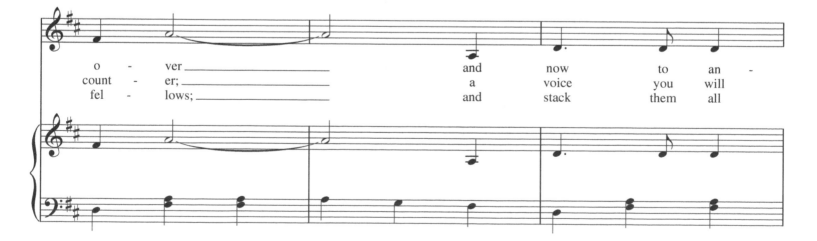

o - ver _____   and   now   to   an -
count - er; _____   a   voice   you   will
fel - lows; _____   and   stack   them all

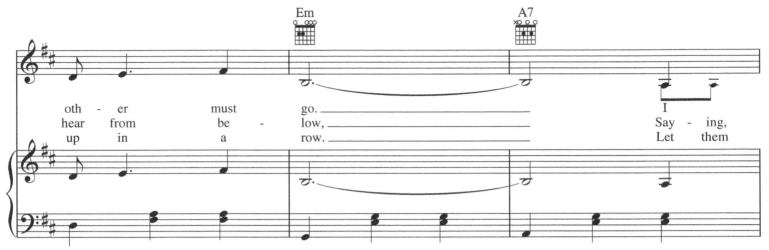

oth - er must go. _____ Say - ing,
hear from be - low, _____ Let them
up in a row. _____

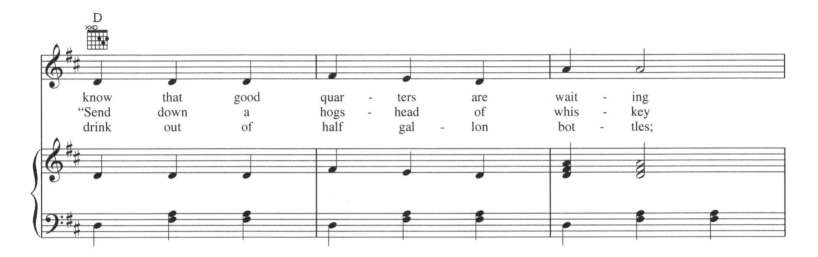

know that good quar - ters are wait - ing
"Send down a hogs - head of whis - key
drink out of half gal - lon bot - tles;

for to wel - come old Ros - in the
to to drink with old Ros - in the
to the mem - 'ry of Ros - in the

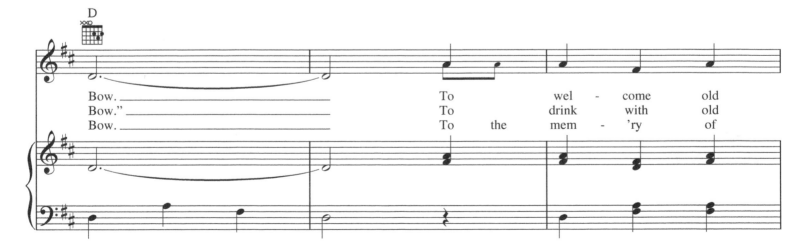

Bow. _____ To wel - come old
Bow." _____ To drink with old
Bow. _____ To the mem - 'ry of

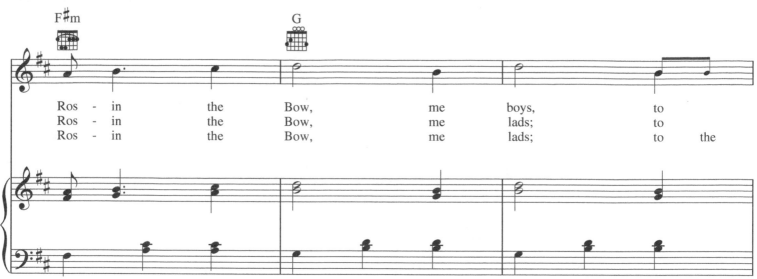

Ros - in the Bow, me boys, to
Ros - in the Bow, me lads; to
Ros - in the Bow, me lads; to the

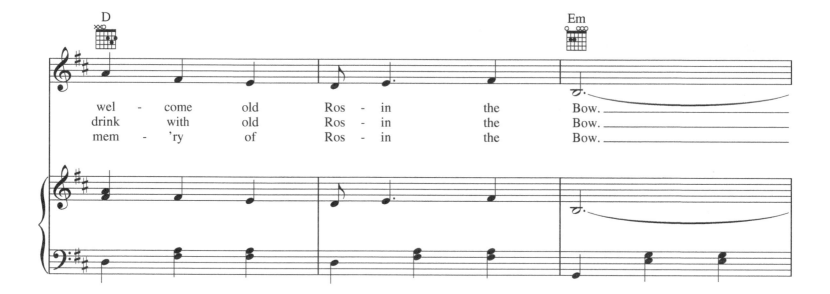

wel - come old Ros - in the Bow.___
drink with old Ros - in the Bow.___
mem - 'ry of Ros - in the Bow.___

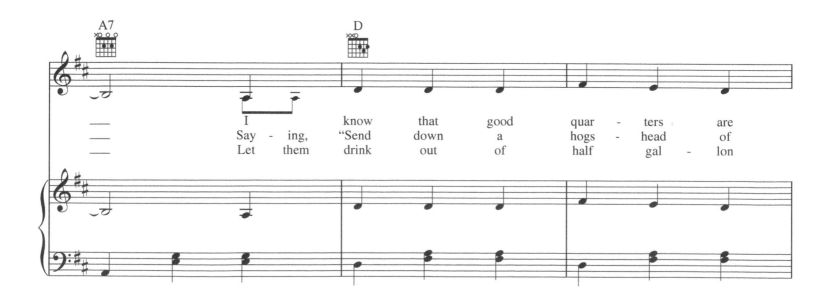

___ I know that good quar - ters are
___ Say - ing, "Send down a hogs - head of
___ Let them Send drink out of half gal - lon

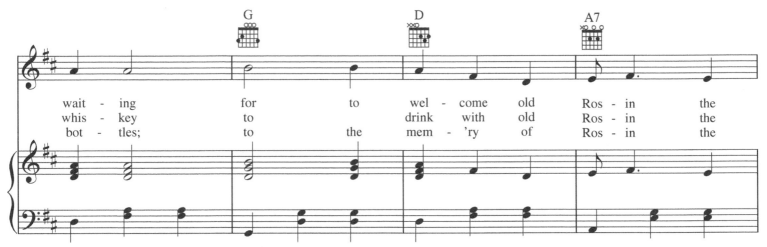

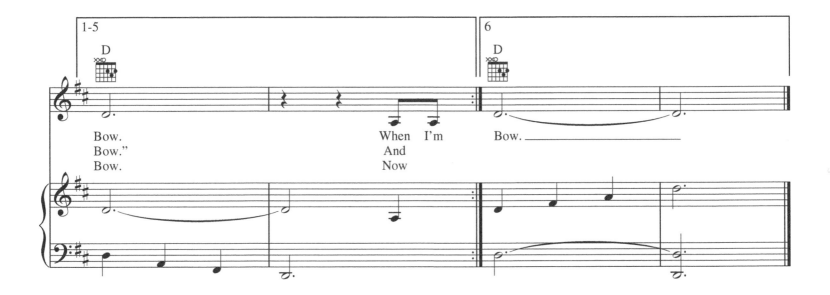

Additional Lyrics

4. Now get this half dozen stout fellows; and let them all stagger and go,
   And dig a great hole in the meadow; and in it put Rosin the Bow.
   And in it put Rosin the Bow, me lads; and in it put Rosin the Bow.
   And dig a great hole in the meadow; and in it put Rosin the Bow.

5. Now get ye a couple of bottles; put one at me head and me toe.
   With a diamond ring scratch out upon them; the name of old Rosin the Bow.
   The name of old Rosin the Bow, me lads; the name of old Rosin the Bow.
   With a diamond ring scratch out upon them; the name of old Rosin the Bow.

6. I feel that old Tyrant approaching; that cruel remorseless old foe.
   Let me lift up my glass in his honour; take a drink with old Rosin the Bow.
   Take a drink with old Rosin the Bow, me lads; take a drink with old Rosin the Bow.
   Let me lift up my glass in his honour; take a drink with old Rosin the Bow.

SAM HALL

Traditional Irish Folk Song

SKIBBEREEN

Traditional Irish Folk Song

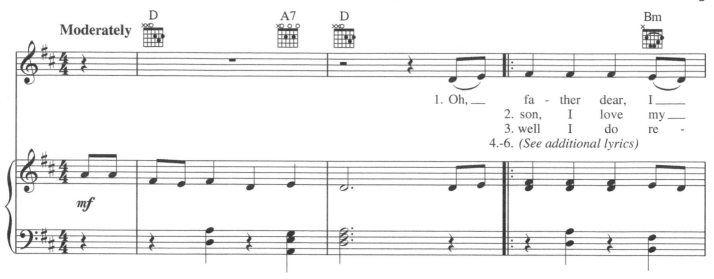

1. Oh, __ fa - ther dear, I __
2. son, I love my __
3. well I do re -
4.-6. *(See additional lyrics)*

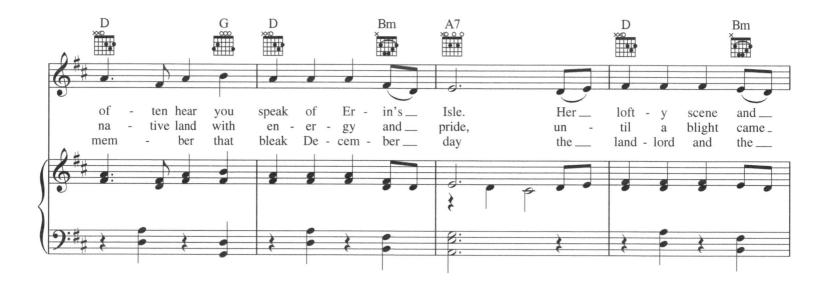

of - ten hear you speak of Er - in's __ Isle. Her __ loft - y scene and __
na - tive land with en - er - gy and __ pride, un - til a blight came __
mem - ber that bleak De - cem - ber __ day the __ land - lord and the __

val - leys green, her moun - tains __ rude and wild. They __ say she is a
on the land, and sheep __ and __ cat - tle died. My __ rent and tax - es
sher - iff came to take __ us __ all a - way. They __ set my roof on

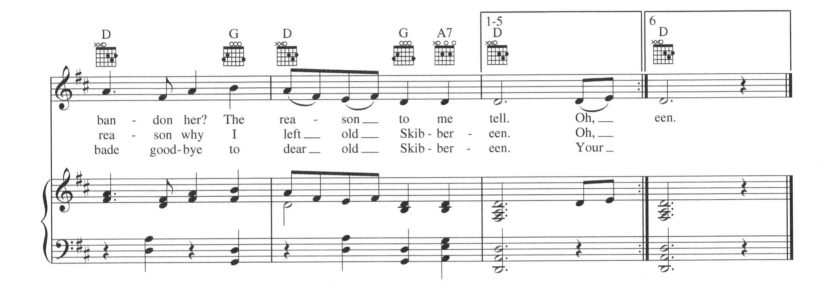

love - ly land, where - in a saint might dwell. So why did you a -
went un-paid, I could not them re - deem. And that's the cru - el
fire with their curs - ed Eng - lish spleen. I heaved a sigh and

ban - don her? The rea - son to me tell. Oh, een.
rea - son why I left old Skib - ber - een. Oh,
bade good-bye to dear old Skib - ber - een. Your

Additional Lyrics

4. Your mother too, God rest her soul, fell on the stony ground.
   She fainted in her anguish, seeing desolation 'round.
   She never rose, but passed away from life to immortal dream.
   She found a quiet grave, me boy, in dear old Skibbereen.

5. And you were only two years old and feeble was your frame;
   I could not leave you with my friends, for you bore your father's name.
   I wrapped you in my cota mor in the dead of night unseen.
   I heaved a sigh and said goodbye to dear old Skibbereen.

6. Oh, father dear, the day will come when, in answer to the call,
   All Irish men of freedom stern will rally one and all.
   I'll be the man to lead the band beneath the flag of green,
   And loud and clear we'll raise the cheer: "Revenge for Skibbereen!"

THE SNOWY-BREASTED PEARL

Irish Folk Song

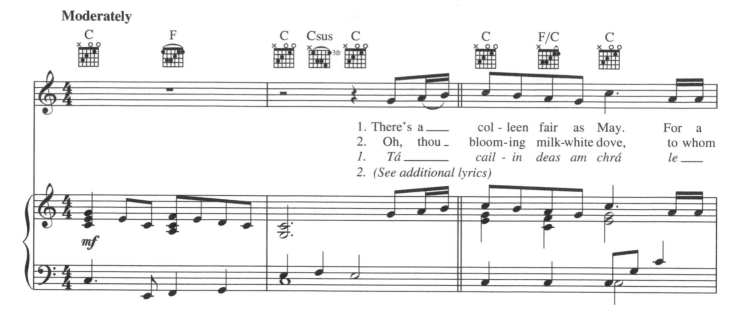

1. There's a ___ col-leen fair as May. For a
2. Oh, thou ___ bloom-ing milk-white dove, to whom
1. Tá ___ cail-in deas am chrá le ___
2. (See additional lyrics)

year and for a day, I have sought by ev-'ry way her heart to gain. There's no ___
I've giv-en true love, do not ev-er thus re-prove my con-stan-cy. There are ___
bliain ag-us le lá, 'S ní fhéad-aim a fáil ___ le bréag - a. Níl ___

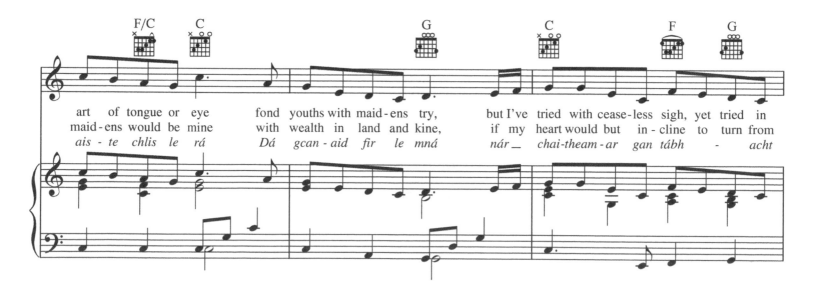

art of tongue or eye fond youths with maid-ens try, but I've tried with cease-less sigh, yet tried in
maid-ens would be mine with wealth in land and kine, if my heart would but in-cline to turn from
ais-te chlis le rá Dá gcan-aid fir le mná nár ___ chai-them-ar gan tábh - acht

vain. If to far off France or Spain she'd cross the wa-ter-y main, to

thee. But a kiss with wel-come bland and touch of thy fair hand are

lé - si. Don Fhrainnc nó don Spáinn dá dtéadh mo ghrá, go

see her face a-gain the seas I'd brave. And if 'tis heav-en's de-cree that

all that I de-mand, wouldst thou not spurn. For if not mine, dear girl, oh

raghainn - se gach lá dá féach - ain. Is mar-an dúinn a - tá i ndán an

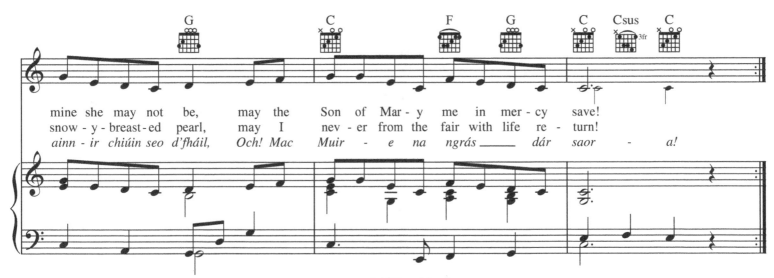

mine she may not be, may the Son of Mar-y me in mer-cy save!

snow-y-breast-ed pearl, may I nev-er from the fair with life re-turn!

ainn - ir chiúin seo d'fháil, Och! Mac Muir - e na ngrás dár saor - a!

Additional Lyrics

2. *Is a chailín chailcee bhláith,*
   Dá dtugas searc is grá,
   Ná túir-se gach tráth dhom éara;
   'S a liacht ainnir mhín im dheáidh
   Le buaibh is maoin 'n-a láimh,
   Dá ngabhaimís it áit-se céile.
   Póg is míle fáilte
   Is barra geal do lámh'
   Sé 'n-iarrfainn-se go bráth mar spré leat;
   'S maran domh-sa taoi tú i ndán,
   A phéarla an bhrollaigh bháin,
   Nár thí mise slán ón aonach!

THE SPANISH LADY

Traditional Irish Folk Song

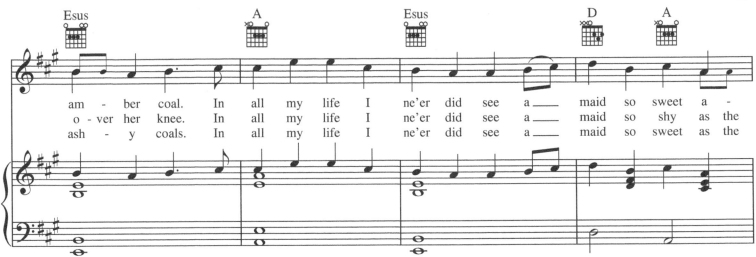

am - ber coal. In all my life I ne'er did see a ___ maid so sweet a -
o - ver her knee. In all my life I ne'er did see a ___ maid so shy as the
ash - y coals. In all my life I ne'er did see a ___ maid so sweet as the

bout the sole.
Span - ish la - dy. Whack fol the too - ra ___ loo - ra, la - dy. Whack fol the too - ra
Span - ish la - dy.

loo - ra - lay. Whack fol the too - ra ___ loo - ra, la - dy. Whack fol the too - ra

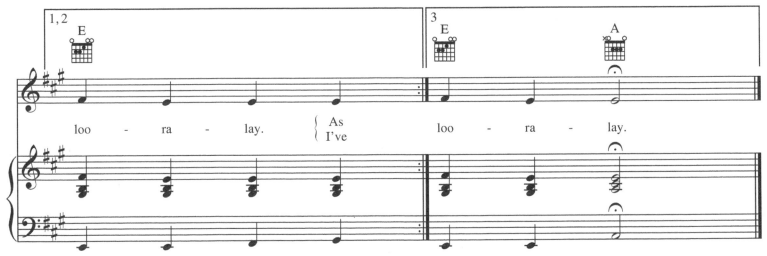

loo - ra - lay. { As } loo - ra - lay.
          { I've }

STAR OF COUNTY DOWN

Traditional Irish Folk Song

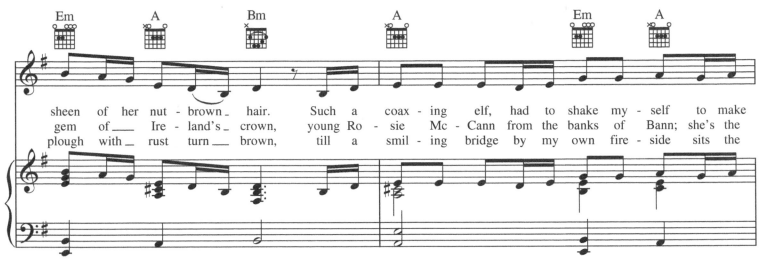

sheen of her nut-brown_ hair. Such a coax-ing elf, had to shake my-self to make
gem of ___ Ire-land's_ crown, young Ro-sie Mc-Cann from the banks of Bann; she's the
plough with_ rust turn ___ brown, till a smil-ing bridge by my own fire-side sits the

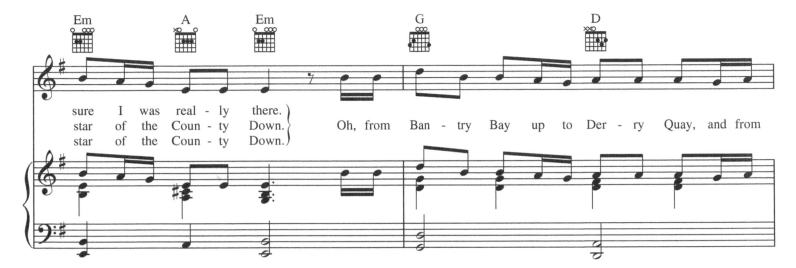

sure I was real-ly there.
star of the Coun-ty Down. } Oh, from Ban-try Bay up to Der-ry Quay, and from
star of the Coun-ty Down.

Gal-way to Dub-lin _ town, no _ maid I've seen like the brown cai-leen that I

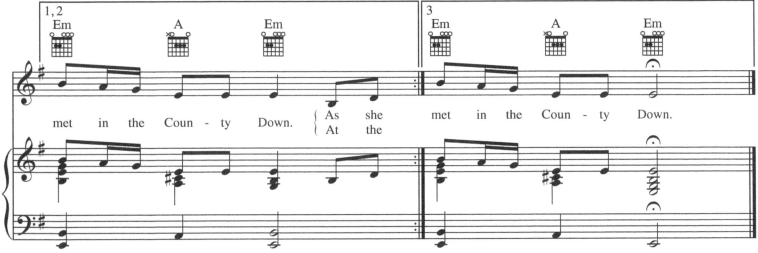

met in the Coun-ty Down. { As she met in the Coun-ty Down.
                          { At the

SWEET CARNLOUGH BAY

Traditional Irish Folk Song

THE WEARING OF THE GREEN

18th Century Irish Folk Song

Spirited

Oh __ Pad - dy dear, and did you hear the
Then __ since the col - or we must wear is
But, __ if at last our col - or should be

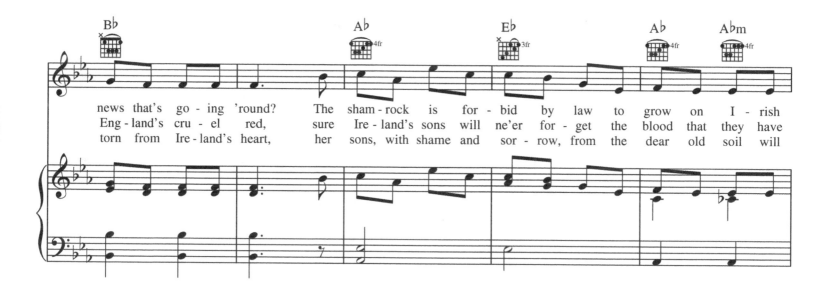

news that's go - ing 'round? The sham - rock is for - bid by law to grow on I - rish
Eng - land's cru - el red, sure Ire - land's sons will ne'er for - get the blood that they have
torn from Ire - land's heart, her sons, with shame and sor - row, from the dear old soil will

ground. Saint __ Pat - rick's Day no more to keep. His col - or can't be seen, for
shed. You may take the sham - rock from your hat and cast it on the sod, but
part. I've heard whis - pers of a coun - try that lies far be - yond the sea, where

THE WILD COLONIAL BOY

Australian Folk Song

Brightly

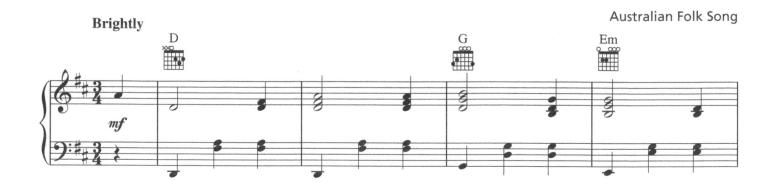

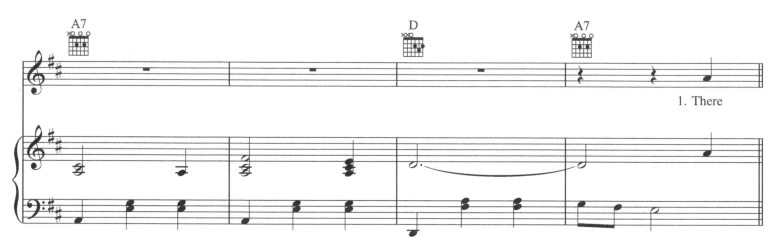

1. There

was   a   wild   co - lo - - - - nial   boy,   Jack
2. ear - ly age   of   six - teen   years,   he
3. two   long years this   dar - - ing   youth   ran
4.-7. *(See additional lyrics)*

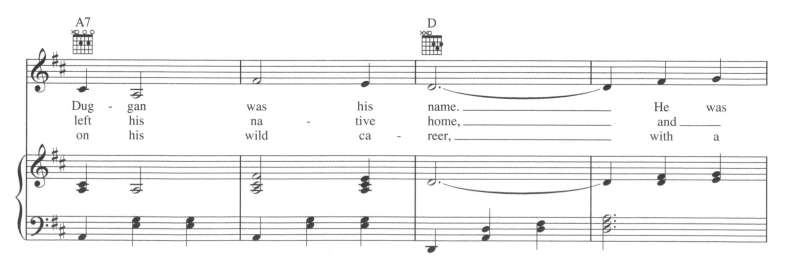

Dug - gan   was   his   name. _____   He   was
left   his   na - tive   home, _____   and _____
on   his   wild   ca - reer, _____   with   a

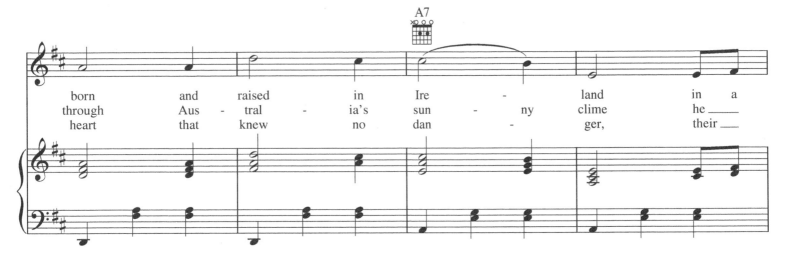

born   and   raised   in   Ire -   land   in a
through   Aus - tral - ia's   sun - ny   clime   he ___
heart   that   knew   no   dan -   ger,   their ___

place   called Cast - le - main. _____   He
was   in - clined   to   roam. _____   He
jus - tice did   not   fear. _____   He

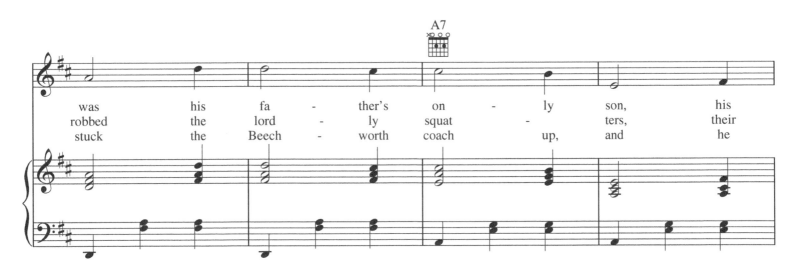

was   his   fa -   ther's   on -   ly   son,   his
robbed   the   lord - ly   squat -   ters,   their
stuck   the   Beech - worth   coach   -   up,   and   he

moth - er's   pride   and   joy, _____   and   dear - ly
flocks   he   would   de - stroy, _____   a   ter - ror
robbed Judge Mc - E - voy, _____   who   trem - bling

did his par - ents love the wild co -
to Aus - tral - ia was the wild co -
gave his gold up to the wild co -

lo - nial boy. At the
lo - nial boy. For
lo - nial boy. He

Additional Lyrics

4. He bade the judge "Good morning" and he told him to beware,
For he never robbed an honest judge what acted "on the square."
Yet you would rob a mother of her son and only joy,
And breed a race of outlaws like the wild colonial boy.

5. One morning on the prairie Wild Jack Duggan rode along,
While listening to the mockingbirds singing a cheerful song.
Out jumped three troopers fierce and grim, Kelly Davis and FitzRoy,
They all set out to capture him, the wild colonial boy.

6. "Surrender now, Jack Duggan, you can see there's three to one,
Surrender in the Queen's name, sir, you are a plundering son."
Jack drew two pistols from his side and glared upon FitzRoy,
"I'll fight, but not surrender," cried the wild colonial boy.

7. He fired point-blank at Kelly and brought him to the ground.
He fired a shot at Davis, too, who fell dead at the sound.
But a bullet pierced his brave young heart from the pistol of FitzRoy,
And that was how they captured him, the wild colonial boy.

WILD ROVER

Traditional Irish Folk Song

Moderately, with a lilt

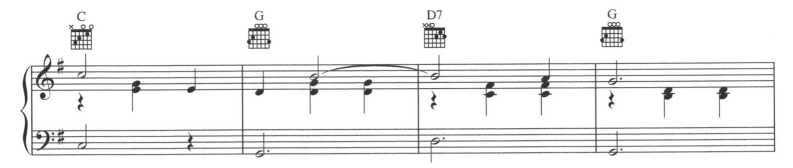

I've been a wild rov - er for man - y a
in - to an ale - house I used to fre -
out of my pock - et I took sov - 'reigns
back to my par - ents, con - fess what I've

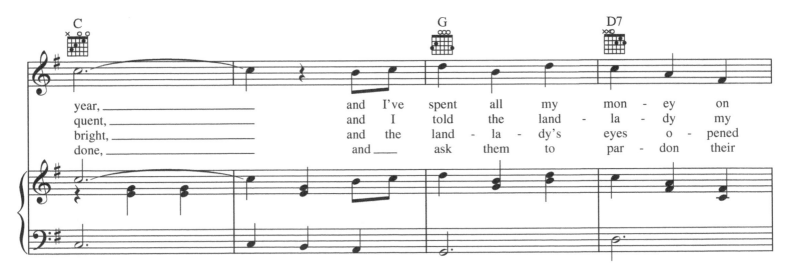

year,_____ and I've spent all my mon - ey on
quent,_____ and I told the land - la - dy my
bright,_____ and the land - la - dy's eyes o - pened
done,_____ and___ ask them to par - don their

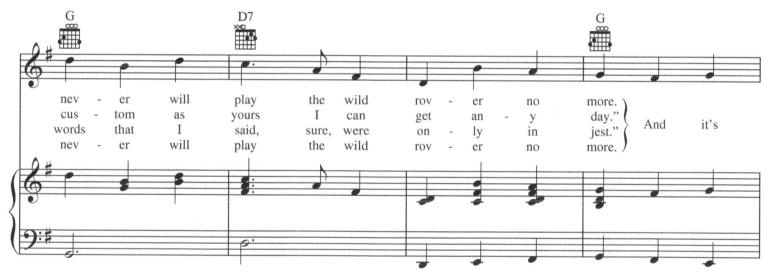

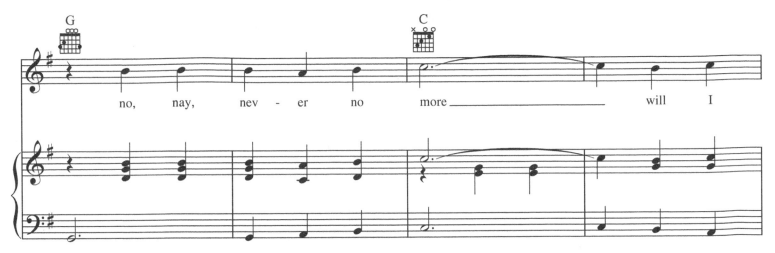

no, nay, nev - er no more _____ will I

play _____ the wild rov - er, _____ no, nev - er _____

no more. _____

I went
Then _ more.
I'll go

8vb

MORE CELTIC & IRISH SONGBOOKS

The popularity of Celtic music has soared over the last decade due to the resurgence of folk instruments, Celtic dancing, and Irish culture overall.

Learn how to play these beloved songs with these great songbooks!

THE BEST OF IRISH MUSIC

80 of the best Irish songs ever written in one comprehensive collection. Includes: Danny Boy • If I Knock the "L" out of Kelly • Macnamara's Band • Molly Malone • My Wild Irish Rose • Peg o' My Heart • Too-Ra-Loo-Ra-Loo-Ral (That's an Irish Lullaby) • Wearin' of the Green • When Irish Eyes Are Smiling • and more.
00315064 P/V/G $16.95

THE BIG BOOK OF IRISH SONGS

A great collection of 75 beloved Irish tunes, from folk songs to Tin Pan Alley favorites! Includes: Erin! Oh Erin! • Father O'Flynn • Finnegan's Wake • I'll Take You Home Again, Kathleen • The Irish Rover • The Irish Washerwoman • Jug of Punch • Kerry Dance • Who Threw the Overalls in Mrs. Murphy's Chowder • Wild Rover • and more.
00310981 P/V/G $19.95

THE CELTIC COLLECTION

The Phillip Keveren Series
Features 15 traditional Irish folk tunes masterfully arranged in Celtic style by the incomparable Phillip Keveren. Songs include: Be Thou My Vision • The Galway Piper • Kitty of Coleraine • The Lark in the Clear Air • Molly Malone (Cockles & Mussels) • and more.
00310549 Piano Solo $12.95

THE GRAND IRISH SONGBOOK

125 cherished folk songs, including: Believe Me, If All Those Endearing Young Charms • The Croppy Boy • Danny Boy • The Galway Races • Johnny, I Hardly Knew You • Jug of Punch • My Wild Irish Rose • Too-Ra-Loo-Ra-Loo-Ral (That's an Irish Lullaby) • The Wearing of the Green • When Irish Eyes Are Smiling • and more.
00311320 P/V/G $19.95

IRISH BALLADS

Nearly 60 traditional Irish ballads, including: Black Velvet Band • Brennan on the Moor • Cliffs of Doneen • Down by the Sally Gardens • I Know My Love • I Never Will Marry • Johnny, I Hardly Knew You • Leaving of Liverpool • Minstrel Boy • Red Is the Rose • When You Were Sweet Sixteen • Wild Rover • and more.
00311322 P/V/G $14.95

IRISH FAVORITES

From sentimental favorites to happy-go-lucky singalongs, this songbook celebrates the Irish cultural heritage of music. 30 songs, including: Danny Boy (Londonderry Air) • The Girl I Left Behind Me • Killarney • My Wild Irish Rose • Tourelay • Who Threw the Overalls in Mistress Murphy's Chowder • and more!
00311615 P/V/G $10.95

IRISH PUB SONGS

Grab a pint and this songbook for an evening of Irish fun! 40 songs, including: All for Me Grog • The Fields of Athenry • I Never Will Marry • I'm a Rover and Seldom Sober • The Irish Rover • Jug of Punch • Leaving of Liverpool • A Nation Once Again • The Rare Ould Times • Whiskey in the Jar • Whiskey, You're the Devil • and more.
00311321 P/V/G $12.95

IRISH SONGS

25 traditional favorites, including: At the Ball of Kirriemuir • At the End of the Rainbow • Dear Old Donegal • Galway Bay • Hannigan's Hooley • The Isle of Innisfree • It's the Same Old Shillelagh • The Moonshiner • The Spinning Wheel • The Whistling Gypsy • Will Ye Go, Lassie, Go • and more.
00311323 P/V/G $12.95

THE CELTIC FAKE BOOK

This amazing collection assembles over 400 songs from Ireland, Scotland and Wales – complete with Gaelic lyrics where applicable – and a pronunciation guide. Titles include: Across the Western Ocean • Along with My Love I'll Go • Altar Isle o' the Sea • Auld Lang Syne • Avondale • The Band Played On • Barbara Allen • Blessing of the Road • The Blue Bells of Scotland • The Bonniest Lass • A Bunch of Thyme • The Chanty That Beguiled the Witch • Columbus Was an Irishman • Danny Boy • Duffy's Blunders • Erin! Oh Erin! • Father Murphy • Finnegan's Wake • The Galway Piper • The Girl I Left Behind Me • Has Anybody Here Seen Kelly • I Know Where I'm Goin' • Irish Rover • Loch Lomond • My Bonnie Lies over the Ocean • The Shores of Amerikay • The Sons of Liberty • Who Threw the Overalls in Mistress Murphy's Chowder • and hundreds more. Also includes many Irish popular songs as a bonus.
00240153 Melody/Lyrics/Chords $25.00

FOR MORE INFORMATION, SEE YOUR LOCAL MUSIC DEALER, OR WRITE TO:

HAL•LEONARD® CORPORATION

7777 W. BLUEMOUND RD. P.O. BOX 13819 MILWAUKEE, WI 53213

Visit Hal Leonard Online at www.halleonard.com

Prices, contents and availability subject to change without notice.

0116